EARLY HOUSES OF NEW ENGLAND

EARLY HOUSES
OF
NEW ENGLAND

by NORMAN B. BAKER

CHARLES E. TUTTLE CO.: PUBLISHERS
Rutland, Vermont

Representatives

Continental Europe: BOXERBOOKS, INC., *Zurich*
British Isles: PRENTICE-HALL INTERNATIONAL, INC., *London*
Australasia: PAUL FLESCH & CO., PTY. LTD., *Melbourne*
Canada: M. G. HURTIG, LTD., *Edmonton*

Published by the Charles E. Tuttle Company, Inc.
of Rutland, Vermont & Tokyo, Japan
with editorial offices at
Suido 1-chome, 2-6, Bunkyo-ku, Tokyo, Japan

Library of Congress Catalog Card No. 67-11935

. *Standard Book No. 8048 0154-1*

First edition, 1967
Second printing, 1970

Book design by Keiko Chiba
PRINTED IN JAPAN

A BOOK OF PLANS AND SKETCHES
INSPIRED BY THE
NEW ENGLAND HOUSES
OF THE 17TH, 18TH & EARLY 19TH CENTURIES
BROUGHT UP TO DATE
FOR MODERN LIVING
By
Norman B. Baker
Drawings and Text by Author
Reviewed by Florence B. Baker
Landscape Architect

TABLE OF CONTENTS

ACKNOWLEDGMENT 11

PREFACE 13

INTRODUCTION 15

    LANDSCAPING 17

    INTERIOR CABINET WORK 18

    EARLY HOUSES 18

OLD NEW ENGLAND HOUSES THAT INSPIRED THE AUTHOR

DRAWING NUMBER		BUILT	PAGE
1–2	McINTIRE GARRISON HOUSE—*Scotland, Maine*	1640	21
3–4	THE BALDWIN HOUSE—*Bradford, Connecticut*	1645	23
5–8	THE WHITMAN HOUSE—*Farmington, Connecticut*	1660	25
9–11	JOHN DILLINGHAM HOUSE—*Brewster, Massachusetts*	1660	29
12–14	CAPT. HAYDEN HOUSE—*Essex, Connecticut*	1665	31
15–16	AULD LANG SYNE HOUSE—*Sconset, Massachusetts*	1675	35
17–18	WILLIAM HARLOW HOUSE—*Plymouth, Massachusetts*	1677	37
19–21	PETER TUFTS HOUSE—*Medford, Massachusetts*	1677	39
22–23	THE CASTLE—*Pigeon Cove, Massachusetts*	1678	41
24–25	OLD GAMBREL LEAN-TO—*Nantucket, Massachusetts*	1689	43
26–27	THE GLEBE HOUSE—*Woodbury, Connecticut*	1690	45
28–29	THE ISRAEL ARNOLD HOUSE—*Lincoln, Rhode Island*	1700	47
30–32	THE THOMPSON HOUSE—*Setauket, L.I., New York*	1700	49
33–34	THE WHITE ELLERY HOUSE—*Gloucester, Massachusetts*	1704	53
35–36	THE ROBINSON HOUSE—*Lanesville, Massachusetts*	1710	55
37–39	THE HAMMOND HOUSE—*Eastville, New York*	1719	57

DRAWING NUMBER		BUILT	PAGE
40	SMALL GABLE LEAN-TO—*Wilton, Connecticut*	1725	59
41–42	THE DENNISON HOUSE—*Annisquam, Massachusetts*	1727	61
43–45	THE MARTIN HOUSE—*Swansea, Cape Cod, Massachusetts*	1728	63
46–47	THE HALLETT-THATCHER HOUSE—*Yarmouth, Massachusetts*	1730	67
48–50	THE SHORT HOUSE—*Newburg, Massachusetts*	1733	69
51–53	THE OLD COLLINS HOUSE—*Gloucester, Massachusetts*	1740	73
54–56	THE VAN DEUSEN HOUSE—*Hurley, New York*	1744	75
57–58	THE OLD GRISWOLD HOUSE—*Guilford, Connecticut*	1750	79
59–61	THE LAURA HOOPER HOUSE—*New Ipswich, New Hampshire*	1752	81
62–63	THE ATWOOD HOUSE—*Chatham, Massachusetts*	1752	83
64–65	THE JOSEPH DAY HOUSE—*W. Springfield, Massachusetts*	1754	85
66–68	THE HENRY HOUSE—*N. Bennington, Vermont*	1769	87
69–70	THE MESSENGER HOUSE—*Harwinton, Connecticut*	1783	91
71–72	THE COL. MEANS HOUSE—*Amherst, New Hampshire*	1785	93
73–74	THE VANDERVEER HOUSE—*Flatbush, L.I., New York*	1787	95
75–76	THE OLD BRICK HOUSE—*Green Mountains, Vermont*	1790	97
77–79	THE GILLIES HOUSE—*Versailles, Connecticut*	1795	99
80–82	THE YOUNG HOUSE—*Chatham Center, New York*	1810–15	101
83	CAPE COD HOUSE—*Little Point St., Essex, Connecticut*	1800	105
84–86	EAST MARION FARMHOUSE—*East Marian, L.I., New York*	1800	107
87–89	THE FALK HOUSE—*Greenlawn, L.I., New York*	1800	109
90	THE GARDEN CITY FARMHOUSE—*Garden City, L.I., New York*	1800	113
91–92	A LONG CAPE COD HOUSE—*Cape Cod, Massachusetts*	1800	115
93	THE OLD STARKEY HOUSE—*Essex, Connecticut*	1800	117
94	27 MAIN ST.—*Essex, Connecticut*	1800	119
95–96	THE DEAN-BARSTON HOUSE—*East Taunton, Massachusetts*	1800	121
97–98	THE HOUSE IN WINDSOR—*Windsor, Connecticut*	1825	123
99–100	THE SWIFT HOUSE—*Oxford, New Hampshire*	1825	125
101	THE BALDWIN HOUSE—*Audubon, New York*	1830	127

DRAWING NUMBER		BUILT	PAGE
102–104	THE PENNY LINCOLN HOUSE—*Scotland, Connecticut*	1835	129
105–106	HOUSE AT LYME—*Lyme, Connecticut*	1800	131
107–108	JUDGE BINGHAM HOUSE—*West Cornwall, Vermont*	1843	133
109–110	BRICK GAMBREL HOUSE—*Farmingham, Connecticut*	1845	135
111	TWO FAMILY HOUSE WITH GARDEN *by Author*		137
112–113	A LONG HOUSE CONNECTED TO BARN *by Author*		139
114–116	A HUDSON RIVER VALLEY BRICK HOUSE *by Author*		141
117	THE AUTHOR'S HOUSE, *Greenlawn, L.I., N.Y., by Author*		143

ACKNOWLEDGMENT

The illustrations and plans of this book were done by the author who has more than sixty years experience as an architect. His association during this time has been with the creative elite of the profession.

The inspiration for the houses of this book was gained from photographs taken from the *White Pine Series or a Series of Architectural Monographs*. This magazine was published six times a year for twenty-five or thirty consecutive years, for the benefit of the profession.

The Series is an intimate treatise of the architecture of the American colonies and of the early Republic presented with admirable completeness to further a broader understanding and to complete a permanent record of the Early American architecture, as stated on the cover of the issue.

Russell E. Whitehead was the editor and George Lindsay and Kenneth Clark furnished measured drawings and beautiful photographs. The text of each number was personally arranged by an important member of the architectural profession.

No greater or more gifted collection of photographs of these beautiful Early American houses can be found.

The author and his wife during their many trips through New England have seen the houses and have been through many of them taking numerous photographs.

The publication of the magazine was done by the White Pine Dealers and Producers of the United States of America and they did a perfect job together with the editor of the magazine.

PREFACE

Many books down through the years have been written describing in detail how these Early American houses were built. Although construction was simple and effective, the method used was as much a matter of expediency as anything else. It is not the intention of the author of this book to go into detail regarding their construction, because it is no longer needed. Rather, it is recommended by the author that if any of the houses pictured in this book were to be built, they should be constructed of braced or balloon frame, using the very best modern methods and material according to the best standard described in the State Building Code. If such does not exist, one should follow the National Building Code, latest edition, taking into consideration this code's provisions for stabilization of the structure against hurricanes and earthquakes.

It is assumed that the owner, when building, will consult an experienced, licensed architect.

Naturally, while as many of the architectural features both inside and out would be retained by the author if he were building, each house would be provided with today's up to date necessities for modern living. However, the old time character of the buildings would be maintained.

Each house listed herein has been inspired by the originals built centuries ago when the country was young and the interior requirements were far simpler than they are at the present time.

In visiting the simple but lovely interiors of these early houses, one almost feels the presence of the pilgrim fathers whose very existence has meant so much to our country, and whose influence has spread over the years throughout the entire country.

INTRODUCTION

Any American who is at all interested in the early history of America, if he or she should stand before the earliest houses described herein, is bound to be impressed by the simplicity, beauty, and strength such houses represent.

Most of these early houses have been restored and preserved through the efforts of just such Americans and as we look out upon so much disorder and uninspired development around us, we feel that it is up to every good American to help in his or her own way to keep the spirit of our early ancestors alive.

The object of this book with its illustrations and text executed by the author is to again try to revive interest in the domestic architecture of the early settlers of New England who came across the ocean from the old country in sailing ships in the year 1620 and thereafter settled on the rugged and wild shores of America. They, with the help of other neighbor settlers, built the homes which inspire this book.

In using these early houses as a suggested basis for modern living, the author had these important ideas in mind. The main body of the houses, especially those of the seventeenth century, represented the beginning of the aesthetic habitation in the New England area. The fact that these houses and those as well of a later period were architecturally good, makes them worthy of reproduction.

By the addition of wings which were not generally a part of the original examples and the rearrangement of the interior layout, not a part of the original but in keeping with it, all was done to provide the buildings with facilities for modern living. It was done in such a way as not to detract from the domestic spirit of the original.

When our forefathers first landed on New England shores, some sort of shelter had to be constructed at once. The male members, many of them craftsmen, built walls of solid saplings cut from wooded sections of the terrain. These were placed at right angles to a cut in the hillside and facing South. Roofs were constructed with saplings tied to the uprights and all joints between the saplings of walls and roofs chinked solidly with clay. Roofs were thatched similar to the roofs of the English countryside. An entrance door in the front and a stone fireplace built across the cut in the hillside furnished the temporary quarters.

There are no remains of these earliest temporary living quarters and within half a century they, according to history, had been replaced with permanent structures, some of which are herein illustrated: beautiful, sturdy and strong and fitted for the needs of the time.

The framework of the houses in the seventeenth century up to many in the early nineteenth century were hewn out of heavy timbers framed and members fitted in advance of erection. One can say that prefabrication is nothing new but started in the early seventeenth century in this country.

Garrison houses, where the walls were built up of solid logs squared on all sides to lay evenly on each other and about seven inches thick, interlocked at the angles and openings and at intersections to hold them in place, were used in many of the very early seventeenth-century houses. Also, the same methods were used in many of the northern New England houses during the French and Indian wars to resist attack and make them less vulnerable to fire. The outside was covered with wood shingles and sometimes with brick for finish.

Garrison buildings housing soldiers during the same period were the origin of such construction.

It should be remembered that the houses of these early days had few if any luxuries which now-a-days are considered essential. Central heating and plumbing systems were unknown. In some cases, if available from some nearby spring, water was brought into the house and allowed to fill a wood storage tank in the kitchen. Otherwise rain water from the roof was brought in and stored the same way. Electric light and wiring for same, bathrooms and their appurtenances, and refrigerators were unknown.

Life was simple and rugged but these very same Americans helped in no small way to make America great and we should be proud of them. They brought with them back in those early days the simple belief that God was with them and would protect them, and that all was right with the country.

Except for a few of the smaller houses it is intended that the houses pictured herein should be given liberal space and except where property is already subdivided in a township, the space given to a home should be not less than two acres. This to prevent future crowding, to give a feeling of space, and to provide for landscape and garden development. Property should always be zoned by the people for their protection. Never build on anything except legally zoned property.

Fireplaces provided the early source of heat and pleasure in the winter. They helped to anchor and stabilize the houses during severe wind storms. This applied especially to the seventeenth-century houses where the large, heavy masonry chimney was located in the center of the house. Fireplaces now-a-days can be equipped with wire mesh drape curtains available anywhere, which completely protect the opening when the fireplace is in use.

The protection which the weight of the heavy central chimney gave to the house of the seventeenth century was clearly demonstrated to the author who with his wife made a trip by car from Long Island to Maine and back in the path of the memorable hurricane on the Atlantic Coast in 1938. Time and again during the length of the trip, we saw houses of modern vintage torn from their foundations. It was not so with the seventeenth- and early eighteenth-century houses. They stood firm on their foundations, held there by their massive stone chimneys and occasionally even supported a high old tree that had been blown over on the house because of the terrific wind.

The eastern end of Long Island was hard hit in this same storm but the old central chimney landmarks, East Hampton's beloved "Home Sweet Home" and the seventeenth-century "John Henry Mulford House," were unharmed.

Naturally the houses would be thoroughly insulated now and the space between frame and window and door frames would be thoroughly caulked with insulation, this being one of the worst places for air leakage in the entire exterior of the wooden home.

Each house would be equipped with a central automatic heating system, combined if desired with an air conditioning system, a properly designed electrical distribution system, and lighting fixtures and outlets. It would also be completely piped with a hot and cold water system, and plumbing fixtures and other equipment as required and selected.

Windows and exterior doors would be completely weather stripped and equipped with storm sash and door—storm sash to match windows and doors.

Above all else it is intended that, though the house be equipped with modern conveniences, in the final appearance the beauty and atmosphere of the original building be maintained.

Such a building of course could only be produced now by an architect having the personal knowledge, experience, and love of the old-time atmosphere and charm that the execution and finish of the houses herein described require.

LANDSCAPING

Proper landscaping is essential to the proper development of any residential property and the author has dared to offer several suggestions as indicated on the various ground plans and property layouts. If the entire property could be landscaped on these sketches, the author would do it, but space does not allow.

The author is a strong believer in the liberal use of trimmed hedges outlining garden areas and enclosing and giving privacy where needed. Such planting ties the house to the ground and presents interesting garden forms so they can be enjoyed in the winter as well as the summer, when the flowers are not in bloom.

The English made good use of trimmed hedges and special specimens and forms to give accent to the gardens. High hedges made a uniform background for the flowers in the beds in front of them. Hedges mean work but they are worth every effort one has to put into them.

Yew, box, holly, privet, beech, hornbeam, laurel, and such were used for the purpose mentioned. Dwarf varieties can be used for bed edges and to accent plants for special purposes where indicated or needed. Evergreen hedges, of course, are much to be desired.

INTERIOR CABINET WORK

Interior wall paneling was used in special rooms, on walls around fireplaces, etc. Such paneling was always found in the early American homes, but it would take a special book to cover the work properly. I suggest that any prospective home builder buy a copy of the book by the well-known author, Samuel Chamberlain, entitled "Beyond New England Thresholds." The book will give all the ideas needed and it should be in every library.

EARLY HOUSES

Generally, except for a few, the main or central body of the original buildings has been maintained for the identification of the type of the early house and the additions by the author are to bring the original house up to date for modern living. In most cases, the actual date when the house was built, as given by the historians, is established and given in the book. Others have been seen and looked over by the author and the date has not actually been established but judged as to vintage by surrounding similar houses in the town or locality. The plate number for each house is herein given consecutively, The history, when available, of the original house and a description of the modifications are made by the author.

EARLY HOUSES OF NEW ENGLAND

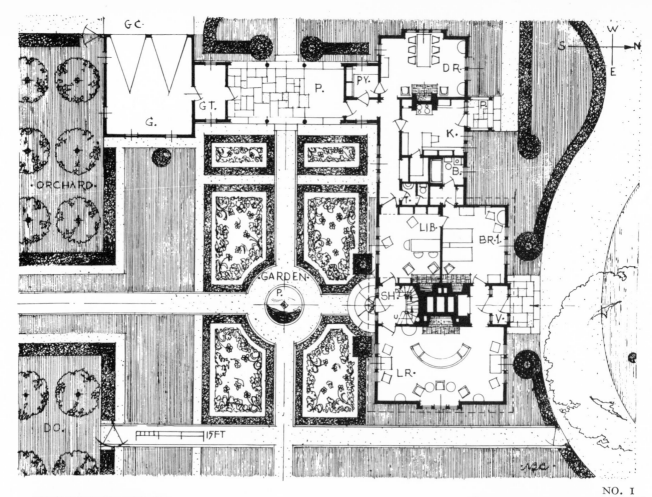

GC.

ORCHARD.

DO.

15 FT

G.C.

G.T.

G.

P.

GARDEN
P.

PY.

DR.

P.

K.

B.

LIB.

BR·1·

SH·

V·

LR·

NO. I

—: GARDEN VIEW PERSPECTIVE :—

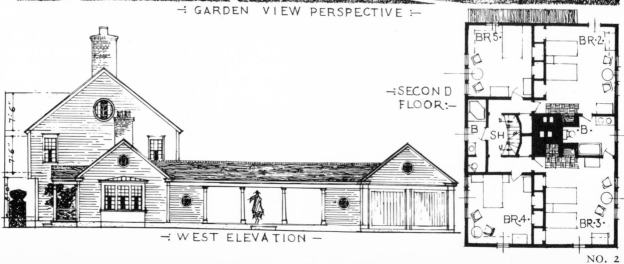

—: SECOND FLOOR :—

BR·5·

BR·2·

B.

SH·

B.

BR·4·

BR·3·

NO. 2

— WEST ELEVATION —

7'·6"

7'·6"

McIntire Garrison House

Scotland, Maine   Original Built 1640

Drawing No. 1 This is the First Floor plan and layout of roads, gardens, and grounds surrounding the house.

The inspiration for this house is the main unit of the McIntire Garrison House in Scotland, Maine, near York. It is a frame-construction and central-chimney house. The second story projects over the First Floor on all sides for defense purposes at that period in our history.

The main section of the house or entrance part contains a Living Room, Library, and Bedroom No. 1 and stairs to Second Floor and to Basement. There is a fireplace in each room of the main section.

A First Floor wing to the west contains a Toilet and Bathroom for Bedroom No. 1, a Kitchen and Entrance Porch to the north, and a Dining Room with Fireplace and Pantry. To the south there is a large Porch giving a broad, general view of a formal garden. A two-car Garage with a separate room for garden tools is on the south end of the wing.

The approach to the house on the north side is by private road to the Main Entrance which extends to the west service road and Garage as indicated on layout.

It is intended that a full-height Basement be provided under the main section of the house with liberal crawl space under the wing.

The "garrison" construction, in the old days which in northern Maine was retained for defense purposes, is described at the beginning of the book under "Introduction."

Drawing No. 2 This drawing shows the plan of the Second Floor containing four Bedrooms and two Bathrooms with Fireplaces for each of the northerly Bedrooms. A Stair Hall is provided with stairs down to the First Floor and up to the Attic which contains a Servant's Bedroom, Bathroom, and Storage Space.

This drawing also contains a perspective view of the house showing the Garden and all of the landscaping, and the relation of the property to the house.

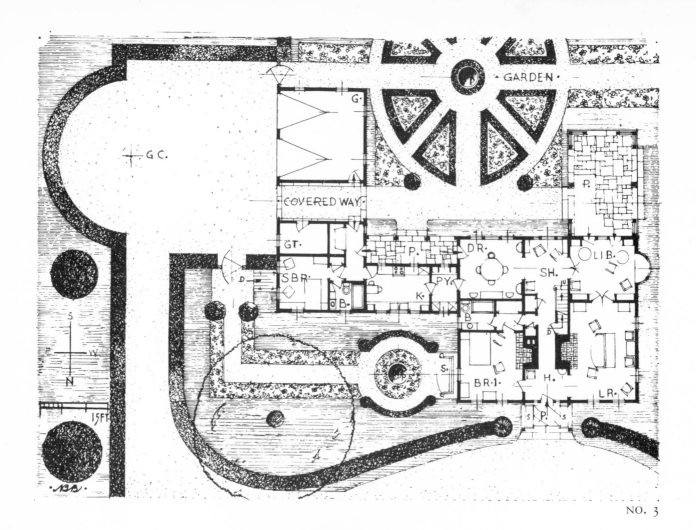

GARDEN

GC

COVERED WAY

G.

GT.

SBR.

D.

B.

P.

K.

DR.

PY.

SH.

LIB.

P.

B.

BR.1.

S.

H.

LR.

P.

S.

S.

NO. 3

NO. 4 ·: PERSPECTIVE :·

B.

L.

SH.

BR.2.

H.

BR.3.

·: SECOND FLOOR :·

·: WEST :·

[22]

THE BALDWIN HOUSE

Bradford, Connecticut   Original Built 1645

Drawing No. 3   This drawing includes the layout of First Floor plan, garden, and grounds. The house was inspired by "The Baldwin House" of Bradford, Connecticut. A frame house, this seventeenth-century edifice is of charming proportions. Liberties were taken by the author in the fenestration and Entrance Porch, north side.

The main house is about square and contains a Central Hall extending through the house. On the west side of the Central Hall a Living Room with fireplace is located with Library to the south and a liberal Porch off the south side of Library. Porches were almost unknown on the old houses of New England because in the early days they offered no protection from Indians or marauders. To the east of the Central Hall is located the Dining Room and a downstairs Bedroom and Bathroom.

To the east the author has added a one-story extension containing Kitchen and Kitchen Porch overlooking the main garden to the south and to the north an interesting, small garden. This wing contains a Pantry between Dining Room and Kitchen and to the east a Servant's Bedroom and Bath. There is a large closet for Kitchen Stores, space for garden tools, and a covered way as entrance to Kitchen also to main formal garden from covered way to south. A Two-car Garage is provided and an ample paved garage court.

In the space between the main porch to the west and Garage Wing to the east a formal garden is formed broken up into box-edged beds with fountain in center.

The approach to the house Entrance is from the north with roads and paths as indicated.

Drawing No. 4   This drawing shows a plan of the Second Floor containing Central Hall (with stairs to First Floor and to Attic storage) and two large Bedrooms with Bath and Toilet. There is a Fireplace in each Bedroom.

The west elevation is indicated on this drawing, drawn to scale and a perspective view of the exterior of the house with private road and land-scaping.

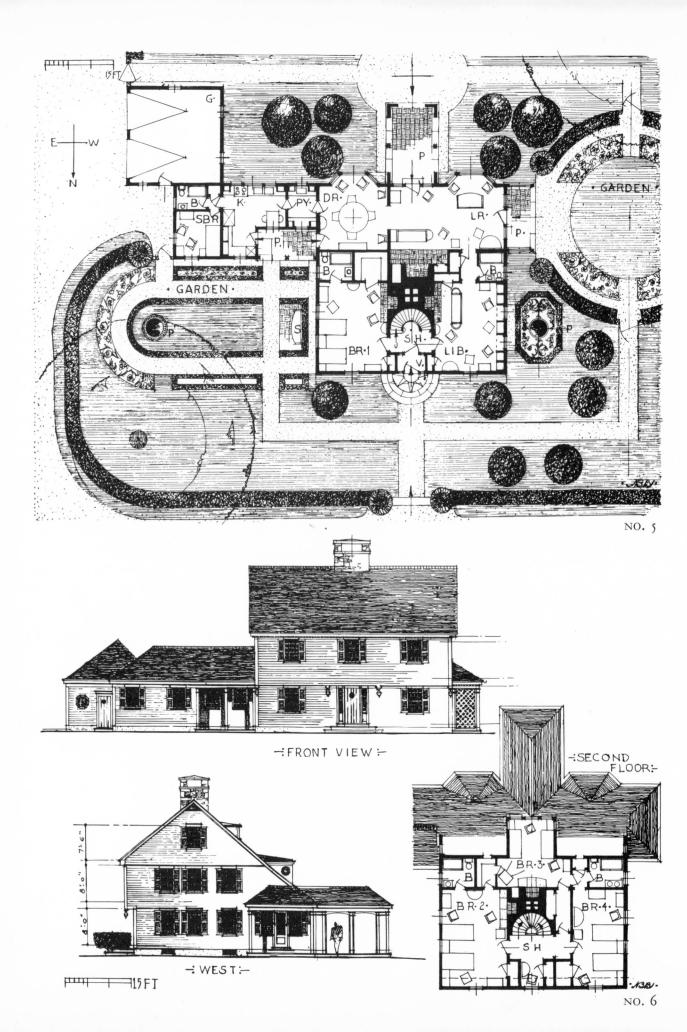

NO. 5

-: FRONT VIEW :-

-: SECOND FLOOR :-

-: WEST :-

15 FT

NO. 6

THE WHITMAN HOUSE

Farmington, Connecticut   Original Built 1660

Drawing No. 5   This drawing is the First Floor Plan and an inspiration of "The Whitman House" located in Farmington, Connecticut. The house is a central, stone-chimney lean-to of frame construction and finish.

The main section is about square, of size indicated. The Main Entrance is of Vestibule Type with half-circle stone steps. The Circular Entrance Hall opening to the west leads to a Library and through a Passage leading to the Living Room on the south. A large Porch leads to the lawn and garden on south side and to a smaller Porch on the west side, which is connected to an ornamental circular garden. A Dining Room opens off the east end of the Living Room.

Bedroom No. 1 and Bath open up to the east from the Stair Hall.

The author has provided a wing to the east containing a small Entrance Porch, Pantry, Kitchen, Servant's Bedroom and Bath, and a Two-car Garage with a Court.

Drawing No. 6   This drawing shows a plan of the Second Floor and contains a Stair Hall with circular stairs, three Bedrooms and two Bathrooms. Fireplaces are provided in Bedrooms No. 2 and No. 3.

This drawing also contains the Front Elevation drawn to scale, and a drawing of the West Elevation drawn to scale.

General Note: It might be interesting to know that this house was featured in an interesting book called "Rooftrees, The Architectural History of an American Family." The author, Philip Lippincott Goodwin, an architect, is well-known and one with whom the author personally has had professional dealings. It is a history of the Goodwin family and the book was copyrighted in 1933 by Philip Lippincott Goodwin, one of the family.

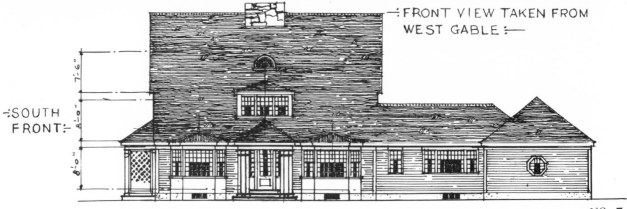

FRONT VIEW TAKEN FROM WEST GABLE

SOUTH FRONT

NO. 7

Drawing No. 7   This drawing pictures the rear elevation with its bay windows from the Living Room and Dining Room as well as the Porch, and the garden and main Porch to the south, drawn to scale.

It also contains a perspective view of the exterior of the house taken from the north side and the west gable.

—: PERSPECTIVE TAKEN FROM EAST GABLE :—
—: SHOWING EAST WING :—

NO. 8

Drawing No. 8   This drawing is a perspective view of the house taken from the north side and showing the east gable, the east or Service wing, the Garage and Entrance, and Garage Court.

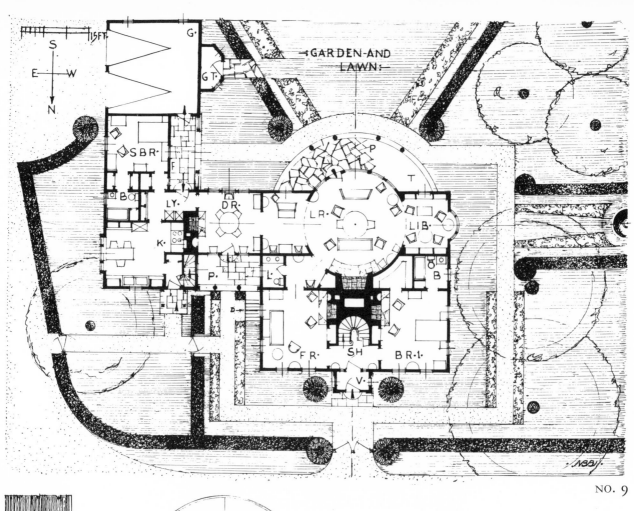

GARDEN·AND
LAWN·

S·BR·2

G·

G·T·

P·

T·

LY·

DR·

LR·

LIB·

K·

B·

P·

L·

FR·

SH·

BR·1·

V·

NO. 9

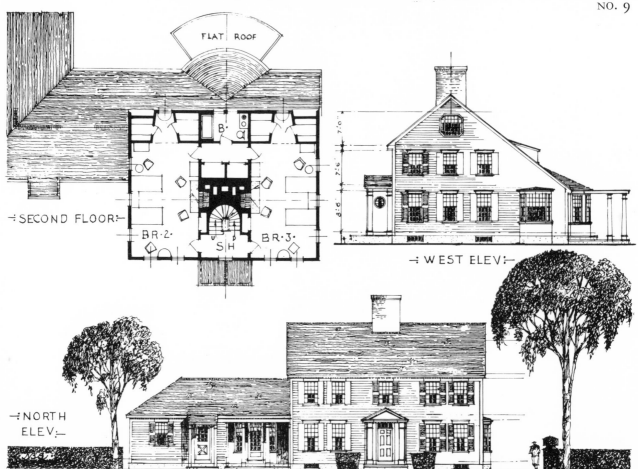

FLAT ROOF

SECOND FLOOR·

B·

BR·2·

SH·

BR·3·

WEST ELEV·

NORTH
ELEV·

NO. 10

John Dillingham House

Brewster, Massachuestts   Original Built 1660

Drawing No. 9   This drawing is the First Floor plan and the inspiration for this house is the main unit of "The John Dillingham House" built at West Brewster, Cape Cod, Massachusetts. The original house was a two-story affair with a central chimney and a lean-to which undoubtedly was built on at a later date.

The First Floor, as designed by the author, contains a Vestibule Entrance leading to circular stairs to the Second Floor. From this Stair Hall on the east side is located a Family Room with Fireplace and Lavatory. It leads to a Living Room with central part circular with a slightly raised ceiling and containing a Central Fireplace. A small Library is at the west end and a Sitting Area at the east end. There is a Dining Room in the east extension with a Fireplace. In the east extension a large Kitchen is provided along with a hooded Entrance with Stairs to Basement and a combination Pantry and Laundry. In the easterly extension running south there is a Servant's Bedroom and Bath, a Porch overlooking the Garden, and a Two-car Garage.

The circular Living Room has a combination Terrace and Porch on the south side overlooking the Garden.

Leading from the Stair Hall on the west side is located Bedroom No. 1 with Fireplace, Bath, and large closet.

Drawing No. 10   This drawing shows the circular Stair Hall and two large Bedrooms and Bath.

This drawing also indicates the Second Floor plan.

The north and west elevations are also shown on this drawing, drawn to scale.

The Attic will provide space for another Bedroom and Bath, and Storage Area.

–: PERSPECTIVE :–

Drawing No. 11   This drawing is a perspective of the exterior of the house as it appears from the northwest. It also indicates the terrain and landscaping.

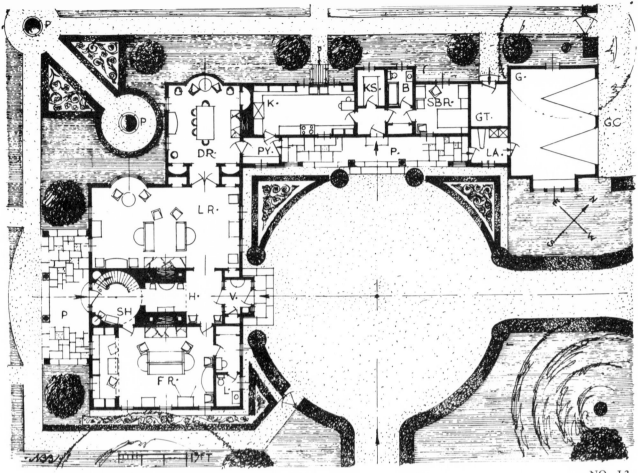

CAPT. HAYDEN HOUSE

Essex, Connecticut   Original Built 1665

Drawing No. 12   This is the First Floor plan and space did not permit the inclusion of the gardens on the northerly and southerly sides but indication has been made on the perspective for this feature.

The inspiration for the main unit is the "Capt. Hayden House" at Essex, Connecticut, which is a fine old house in a fine old New England town. Essex is a town the author is very fond of for in addition to the wonderful colonial atmosphere he designed a house there for lifelong friends and much of the inspiration for this book was derived from Essex and the surrounding countryside.

As one can see, it is a liberal plan. The house is approached by a private road to a large, circular, hedged in area formed by the main two-story, central-

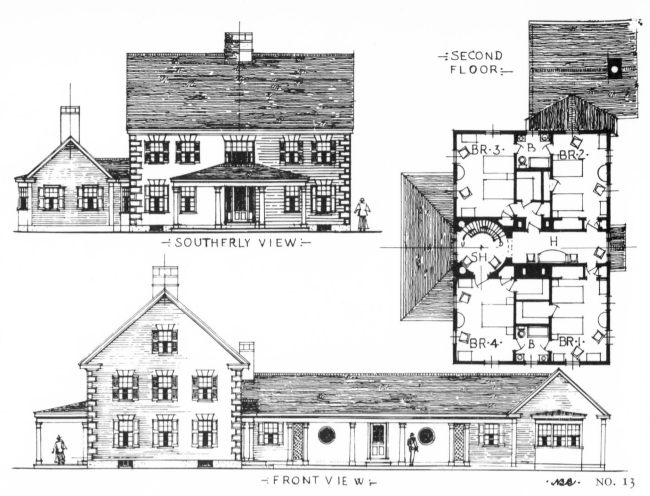

-: SECOND FLOOR :-

BR·3· | B | BR·2·

SH | H

BR·4· | B | BR·1·

-: SOUTHERLY VIEW :-

-: FRONT VIEW :-   NO. 13

-: PERSPECTIVE :-   NO. 14

chimney unit on the southerly side, and the one-story wing running northerly to a two-story garage and court.

The main unit First Floor is composed of a Vestibule Entrance leading to a Central Stair Hall with a radial Stair Hall at the southerly end of the Hall. At the westerly side of the hall is located a large Family Room with a Library Alcove on the southerly end. A Coat and Powder Room are on the northerly end of this room.

A roomy Porch overlooking a formal Garden with a fountain is on southerly side as indicated on perspective.

From the Hall, the Living Room is on the easterly side of the main unit. Both the Family Room and the Living Room are provided with large fireplaces.

The one-story extension on the easterly side of the main unit contains a large Dining Room with fireplace and an entrance to the Living Room. A large Kitchen has a Pantry to the Dining Room. The Kitchen Stores, the Servant's Bedroom and Bath, a small laundry, Room for garden tools, and a two-car Garage are on the northerly end with Paved Court. A long Porch extends from the Pantry to the Laundry.

On the easterly side of the one-story wing is located a large vegetable garden and a formal, cutting-flower garden.

Drawing No. 13   This drawing contains the Second Floor plan with Hall through the center of the two-story main unit. Stairs are on southerly end and corner cabinets as indicated. On each side of the Hall are located two large Bedrooms and Bathrooms.

The circular stair leads to the Attic Floor where two Rooms and Bath can be provided, if desired.

The drawing also indicates the southerly view with large Porch and triple windows in circular Stair Hall and the end of the easterly one-story wing.

This drawing shows the special trim required. In addition to wood cornices and siding, the house is further added to by the introduction of a special wood quoins and segmental arches over the windows, and other decorative details.

Drawing No. 14   This drawing indicates a perspective view of the house taken from the air and indicates in this way the gardens to the south and to the north as heretofore mentioned. It also indicates the terrain and the landscaping.

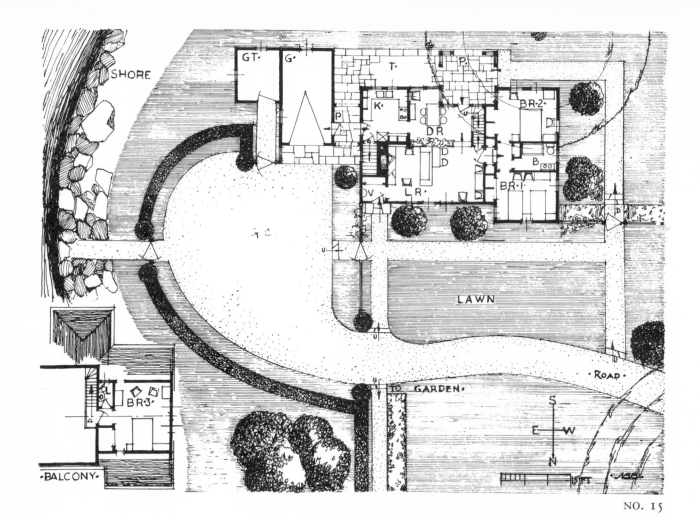

SHORE

GT. G.

T. P.

P. K. BR·2·

DR B

LR· BR·1

OV

LAWN

ROAD

BR·3·

BALCONY

TO GARDEN

S
E W
N

NO. 15

·FRONT VIEW PERSPECTIVE·

·SECTION· ·REAR VIEW·

NO. 16

ᴀ̀ULD LANG SYNE HOUSE

Sconset, Massachusetts   Original Built 1675

Drawing No. 15   This drawing shows a seashore cottage of simple proportions, a beach, presumably at Sconset, Massachusetts, and treatment of grounds. It does not show the garden for lack of space. It is located by the author on a seashore promontory and the inspiration for the house is the "Auld Lang Syne House" of Sconset.

The First Floor plan indicates a Vestibule Entrance to the Living Room with a fireplace, a Dining Room down two steps to a Porch on the south with Terrace facing the water and a distant view. The Kitchen has an inside entrance to the Basement and from the Kitchen through a covered Porch to the Garage and Room for Garden Tools.

Off the Living Room are provided two Bedrooms and Bath. The ceiling of the Living and Dining Rooms is formed by roof rafters with decorative truss as indicated.

There is access from the stairs to a Mezzanine Bedroom and Bath overlooking the Living Room as indicated.

Drawing No. 16   This drawing is a Front View of the house, a Cross Section through the house at the Dining Room and Living Room levels. There are stairs leading to the Mezzanine Bedroom.

Also as indicated, a perspective of the exterior of the house from the northwest.

The chimney is brick, the exterior walls are shingles, all painted white. The Living Room and Dining Room are paneled and stained.

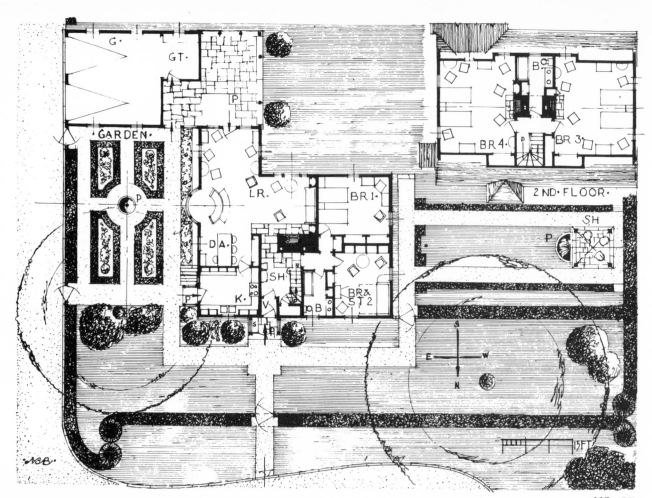

GARDEN

G.
GT.
P

LR.

DA.
K.
P
SH.
V
B
BR 1.
BR & ST 2
SH
P

BR 4
BR 3
B
D
2ND·FLOOR·

15 FT

NO. 17

WEST ELEV.

PERSPECTIVE

NO. 18

WILLIAM HARLOW HOUSE

Plymouth, Massachusetts   Original Built 1677

Drawing No. 17   This drawing shows the First and Second Floor plans and part of the land-scaping of grounds. The approach to the house is by private road leading to the house and continuing around to a two-car Garage as indicated. It is a compact plan.

The house has a single chimney and a gambrel roof for the main house and the wing has a ridge roof, walls of clapboarding. This is inspired by the "William Harlow House" of Plymouth, Massachusetts, and is, according to history, the second oldest house in the town. The author was informed that it was built after the close of the King Philips War. The timbers, the local historians say, were taken from the fort on Burial Hill, which was abandoned when the fighting ceased. It is now the property of the Plymouth Antiquarian Society. The author was architect for a house just like the main unit, in West-bury, Long Island, New York, for one of his daughters.

The First Floor contains a large L-shaped Living Room with fireplace and on the north end a Dining Alcove which leads to the Kitchen and Kitchen Entrance Porch from outside. At southerly end the Living Room is connected to a Porch and a Two-car Garage with space for garden tools. There is a one-story Addition east and west.

A formal garden with fountain can be admired from the Dining Alcove and the Living Room. From the Stair Hall there are two Bedrooms and Bath. From these Bedrooms a long hedged-in garden with a Summer House at the westerly end can be observed—a pleasure to be contemplated.

On the same drawing a Second Floor plan has been drawn, providing two large Bedrooms with Fireplaces and Bathroom as indicated.

Drawing No. 18   This drawing contains a west elevation and a perspective view of the exterior of the house including the site, landscaping, and road.

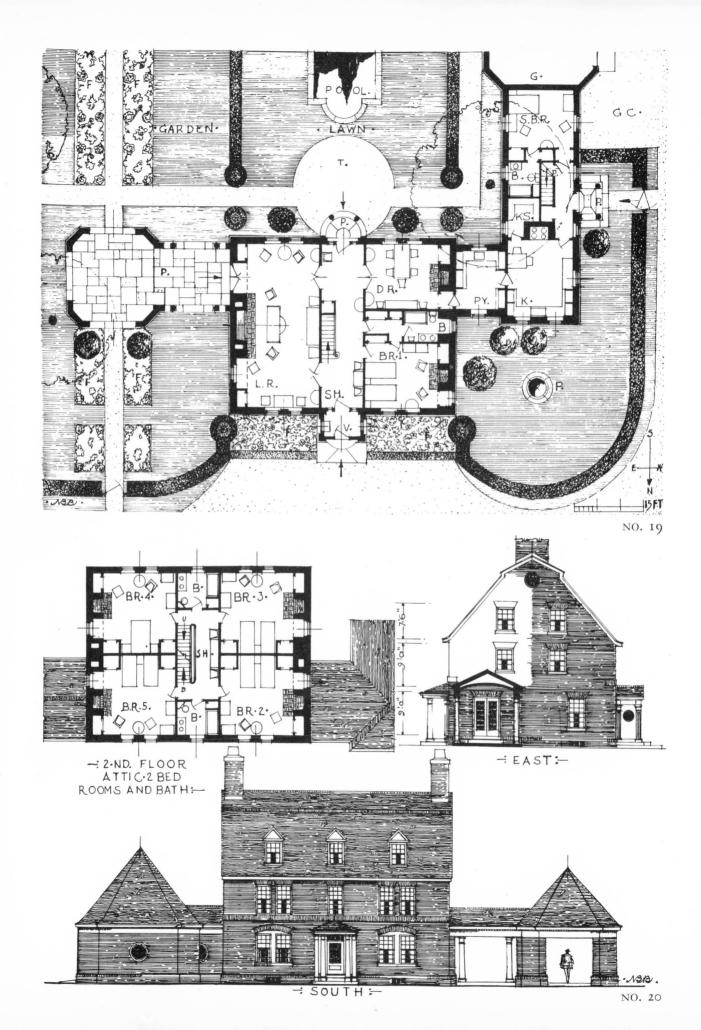

F · · F
GARDEN ·
LAWN ·
POOL.
G.
G C ·
S. B. R.
B.
KS.
T.
P.
P.
DR.
PY.
K.
P.
B.
L.R.
BR.1.
P
SH.
V.
F
S
E
N
15 FT
NO. 19

BR·4.
B·
BR·3.
U
SH·
D
B.R.5.
B·
BR·2.

·2·ND· FLOOR
ATTIC·2 BED
ROOMS AND BATH·

76"
9.0"
9.0"

· EAST ·

· SOUTH ·

NO. 20

PETER TUFTS HOUSE

Medford, Massachusetts   Original Built 1677

Drawing No. 19   This drawing shows an early brick masonry house. The inspiration for the two-story and Attic unit is the "Peter Tufts House" at Medford, Massachusetts, built, it is told, in the year 1677. It has been modified slightly by the author to include a Service Wing to the west and a large wing containing a spacious Porch on the east. The house is a gambrel roof type with a chimney at each gable end.

It is approached by private drive from the main road. There is a Vestibule Entrance decorated on each side by a hedged in bed of perennial flowers to provide contrasting colors.

A Stair Hall runs through the house to a small circular entrance to the south and beyond the terrace is a lawn and flower bordered pool. To the east, off the central hall, there is a Living Room the full width of the house with a large fireplace, and an access to the one-story exterior Porch extension. To the west are Bedroom No. 1 and Bath and the Dining Room which overlooks the Garden. From the Dining Room the westerly, one-story Service Wing is provided running north and south and laid out as indicated. The Bedroom and the Dining Room both have fireplaces.

The private road extends to the west to a two-car Garage with Garage Court.

Drawing No. 20   This drawing indicates the Second Floor layout containing four Bedrooms with fireplaces and two Bathrooms and Stairs to Storage Attic.

Also shown are the east and south elevations. The brick walls inside are furred and plastered. Arch brick is ground to proper shape. Band at Second Floor is to be laid the eight-inch way; special dentilated wood cornice where indicated; roof, slate; doors and windows, wood.

NO. 21

Drawing No. 21   This drawing is a perspective view of the exterior of the house looking from the northwest and indicating landscape and possible countryside.

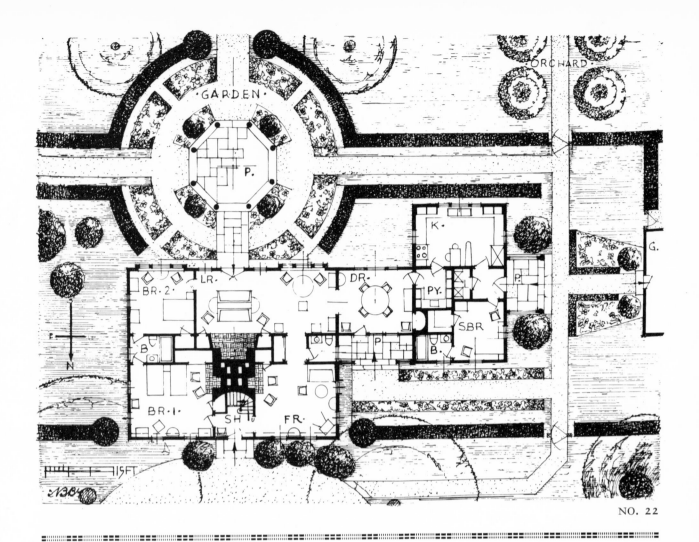

THE CASTLE

Pigeon Cove, Massachusetts   Original Built 1678

Drawing No. 22   This drawing describes the First Floor plan. The inspiration for this house was the main unit of what was years ago known as "The Castle" located at Pigeon Cove, Massachusetts. It is a central, stone-chimney house of wood-frame construction finished on the outside with clapboarding. It is a two-story, attic type and the Second Story projects beyond the First Floor on the north front. There is a lean-to at the rear evidently built at a later date because of different pitch.

There is an Entrance door to a small Stair Hall and on the east side there are two Bedrooms with a Bath between. There is a fireplace in the northerly Bedroom. On the west side there is a Family Room with fireplace. To the south of this room there is a large Living Room with double doors leading to an outdoor, freestanding Porch in the center of a formal garden. Off the Living

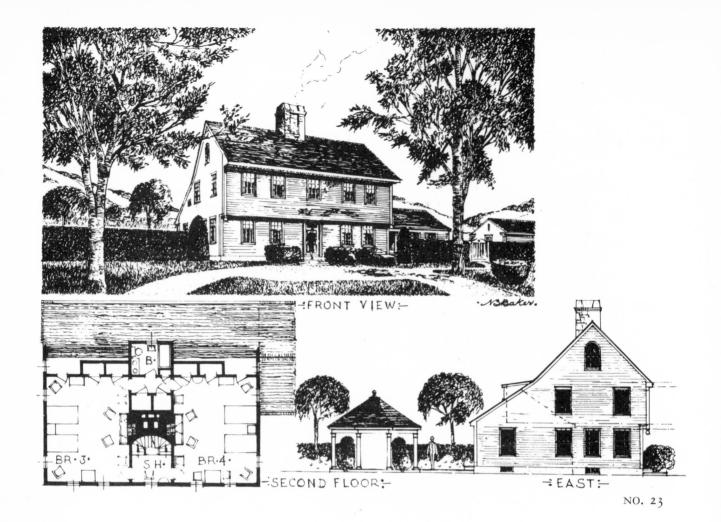

‡FRONT VIEW‡

‡SECOND FLOOR‡

‡EAST‡

BR·3·   SH   BR·4·

NO. 23

Room there is a one-story extension to the west with a large Pantry and Kitchen, a small Laundry, and a Servant's Bedroom and Bath, with Service Entry and Porch. A path leads to separate two-car Garage with paved court and roadway connecting to the house.

Drawing No. 23   This drawing includes a Second Floor plan containing two large Bedrooms with fireplaces and a Bathroom to the south. Also included are the easterly elevation showing a free-standing Summer House in the Garden and a perspective view of the exterior of the house drawn from the northeast side.

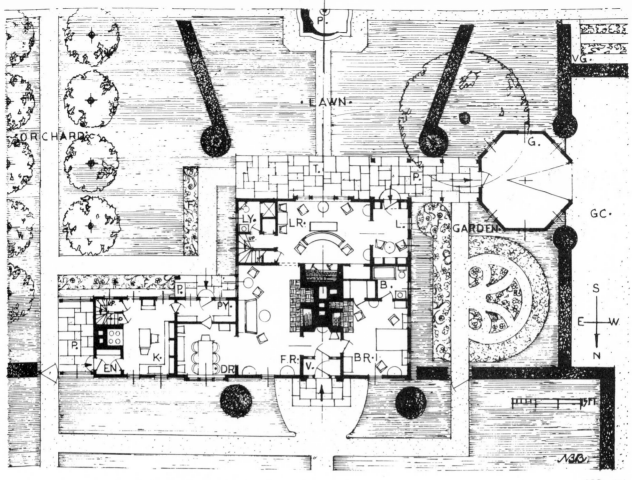

OLD GAMBREL LEAN-TO

Nantucket, Massachusetts Original Built 1689

Drawing No. 24 This drawing indicates a First Floor plan of a low, intimate, story-and-a-half lean-to, single-chimney frame house. This is inspired by a house on Pine Street, Nantucket, Massachusetts. Nantucket is an island off the coast, swept by the sea and is crowded with Early Americana. The author has no name for this house but undoubtedly it has one somewhere. It was built in the year 1689. Because of its distinctive roof design, let's call it, "The Old Gambrel Lean-to."

The main unit of the house is about square and while the original house has four windows on the front the author has placed only two. The First Floor of the main unit contains a Family Room opening on to a Living Room to the south together with a small Library. One enters the house from a private drive and a Vestibule Entrance from the north.

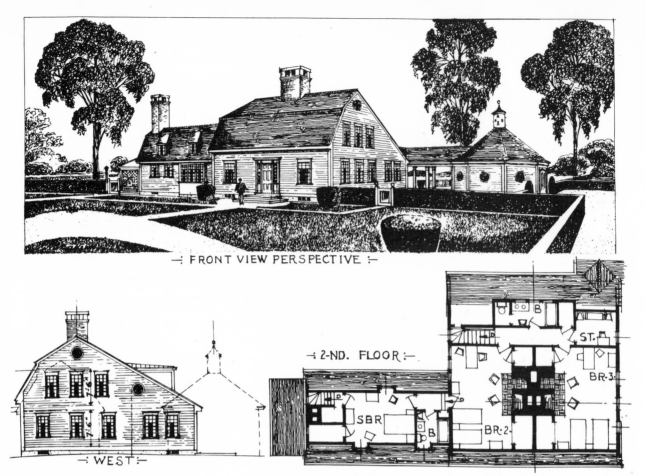

-: FRONT VIEW PERSPECTIVE :-

-: WEST :-

-: 2-ND. FLOOR :-

NO. 25

The stairs to Second Floor and to the Basement are located on the south-easterly end of the main unit as is the Lavatory with shower.

The author has introduced a one-story wing to the west with Entrance to Porch and Terrace from the Library end of the Living Room. At the end of the Porch there is a single-car Garage. Outside of Bedroom No. 1 there is a small formal garden and on axis with the Living Room there is a large lawn with a pool and fountain.

To the east there is a story-and-a-half addition containing a Dining Room with a Bay, Pantry and Porch, and Stairs to the Servant's Bedroom and Bath on the floor above.

Drawing No. 25 This drawing contains a Second Floor plan with two large Bedrooms with fireplaces, a Bathroom, a small Study, and Stair Hall to the First Floor. In the attic of the extension to the east, a Servant's Bedroom and Bath are located, lighted and ventilated by dormer windows. A small stairway leads down to the Kitchen. This area has access to Bedroom No. 2 which may be used for storage.

This drawing also contains a west elevation and a perspective drawing of the house from the outside taken from a northwest angle. The composition of this small house is good.

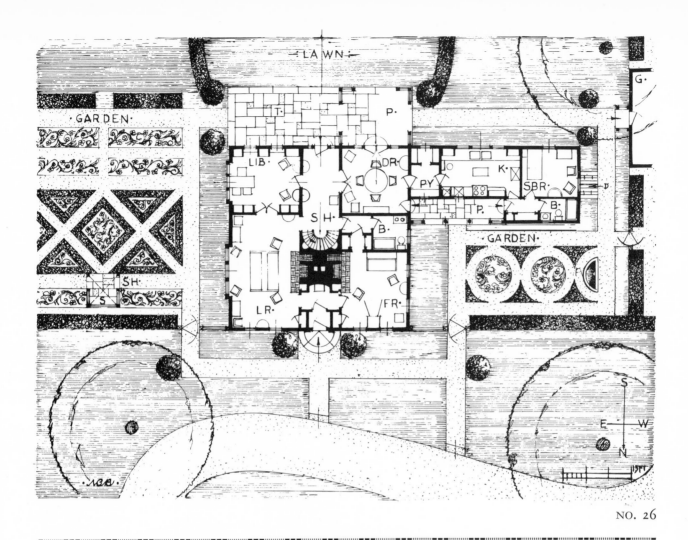

THE GLEBE HOUSE

Woodbury, Connecticut   Original Built 1690

Drawing No. 26   This drawing is the First Floor plan. The inspiration for the main unit is "The Glebe House," known as the birthplace of American Episcopacy since the First Episcopalian in America, Samuel Seabury, was elected here. It is a gambrel lean-to.

Approaching by a private road, the house is entered through a vestibule. To the east, one enters a Living Room with a fireplace. A Library is on the south. A circular stair in a southerly Hall gives access to a Dining Room. A Porch and Terrace the full width of the main unit is provided. From the front Hall to the west is a Family Room with fireplace and a downstairs Bath is also off the Hall.

To provide the necessary conveniences the author has included a one-story

-: PERSPECTIVE :-

-: SECOND FLOOR :-

NO. 27

high extension to the west with a Pantry and Kitchen and Front Porch. Also, a Servant's Bedroom and Bath are included in the plan.

A separate two-car Garage has been provided at the west end.

A formal, hedged garden with Summer House is the main attraction from the Living Room and Library to the east. A hedge-enclosed lawn area extends from the Terrace and Porch to the south and a small hedged formal garden with pool is visible from the Family and Dining Rooms to the west.

Drawing No. 27 This drawing is the Second Floor plan containing four Bedrooms. Bedrooms No. 1 and No. 2 have fireplaces. Two Bathrooms are provided; also, a Stair Hall with circular staircase.

There is also shown a rendered perspective view of the exterior of the house taken from the northwest which indicates the privacy obtained by a completely hedged in enclosure both summer and winter.

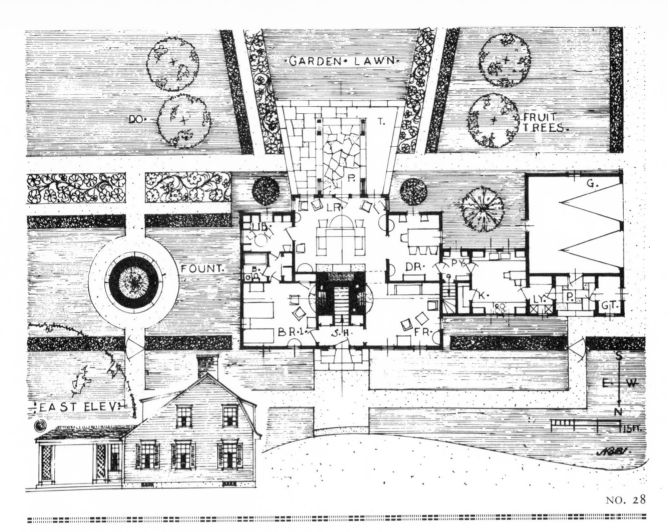

GARDEN · LAWN.

DO.

FRUIT TREES

FOUNT.

EAST ELEV.

NO. 28

THE ISRAEL ARNOLD HOUSE

Lincoln, Rhode Island   Original Built 1700

Drawing No. 28   This house is about the same in size as drawings No. 24 and No. 25 of the old gambrel roof house in Nantucket and it is just about as intimate. The addition of two more windows on the First Floor front and the two dormer windows in the roof of the Second Floor front makes the difference.

The inspiration for the house is the "Israel Arnold House" of Lincoln, Rhode Island.

The First Floor plan shows a small Entrance in the stairs to the Second Floor running up from the Entrance Hall between the chimneys as they sometimes did in those days. To the west of this Hall is a fairly large Family Room. This leads to the Living Room; also to a Library to the southeast and to a Dining Room to the southwest. A large fireplace is provided in the Living Room. The stair to the Second Story runs up over the fireplace but a smoke chamber and flue is designed so as not to interfere.

-: PERSPECTIVE :-

2ND. FLOOR PLAN

-: FRONT ELEVATION :-

NO. 29

The Living Room opens out onto a combination covered Terrace and Porch and beyond overlooks a hedged informal garden. To the east, the Library and Bedroom No. 1 overlook a hedged in fountain the spray of which is controlled and operated by a small hydromatic pump re-circulating the water.

To the west there is a one-story addition containing a Pantry, inside stair to Basement under main house unit and a Kitchen. The Laundry, Garden tool space, a small Porch and a two-story Garage are also provided.

This drawing also contains the east Elevation of the extension of the house drawn to scale.

Drawing No. 29 This drawing shows the Second Floor plan which contains two large Bedrooms with a fireplace in each and a Bath for the two rooms.

The front or north elevation is also indicated. The walls of the exterior are finished with clapboarding except for the walls of the recessed Porch and north and south pediments of Garage. These are finished with flush T and G pine boarding.

A perspective is also provided on this drawing showing the exterior of the house as seen from the northeast and a possible exterior setting for the house and the landscaping.

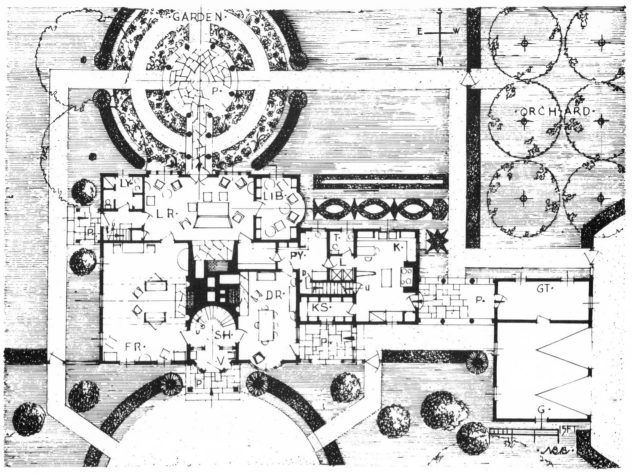

THE THOMPSON HOUSE

Setauket, L.I., New York　　　Original Built 1700

Drawing No. 30　　This house is inspired by "Thompson Home" at Setauket, built in the year 1700 on Long Island, New York, not far from the author's home. The main unit is a lean-to with seven windows, the front facing the north. There is an addition with a gabled roof containing the Service Area. The author has extended the building by a Porch from the Kitchen to a two-car Garage. The paved Garage road is a part of the private road connecting with the Entrance Court which is surrounded by a hedge.

The First Floor is entered from the north through a lean-to, latticed Porch and Vestibule to a Stair Hall with circular stairs to the Second Floor. To the east one enters a large Family Room with fireplace which adjoins the Living Room to the south. This also has a large fireplace exhausting through a central chimney. To the east there is another Stair Hall to the Second Floor,

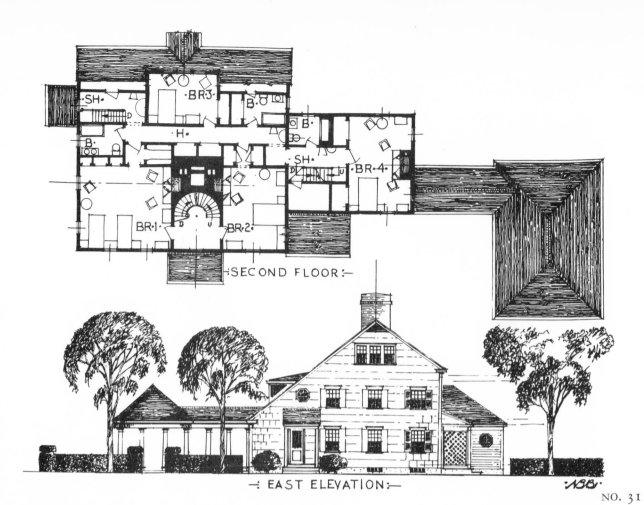

=SECOND FLOOR=

=EAST ELEVATION=

·NBB·

NO. 31

=PERSPECTIVE=

·NBBaker·

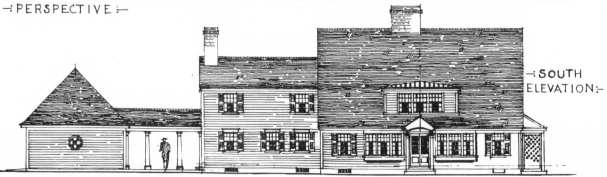

=SOUTH ELEVATION=

NO. 32

a Lavatory, and a small outside Porch. At the west end of the Living Room there is a small Library with a bay window looking out on a decorative, hedged garden. To the west of Entrance Stair Hall there is a large Dining Room with a fireplace and exit to a small Porch. The Service Wing contains a Pantry, Kitchen Stores, Laundry and Service toilet, and also a large Kitchen and Stairs to Basement and to the Second Floor. This wing also connects to a Porch and two-car Garage with space for Garden tools.

Off the south from the Living Room there is a circular arbor set in the center of an attractive round, hedge-enclosed garden. Off the south of the Garage wing there has been provided a space for an orchard and farther to the south a vegetable garden.

Drawing No. 31 This drawing contains a Second Floor plan covering the main unit and the Kitchen Extension. It shows also four family Bedrooms and three Bathrooms. The Main and Service Stairs extend up to the Third or Attic Floor where a family Bedroom and Bath can be provided. A Servant's Bedroom and Bath is located with access from the Service Stairs. The Main Stairs on the north side of the Main unit could, if so desired, be omitted from the Second to Attic Floor.

This drawing also indicates the easterly elevation and circular Porch.

The east and west ends of main unit are shingled with large cedar shingles and the remainder of facing is finished with narrow pine clapboarding as indicated.

Drawing No. 32 This drawing indicates the rear or south elevation, fenestration and finish; also a perspective view of the house taken from the north and indicating the landscaping and possible countryside.

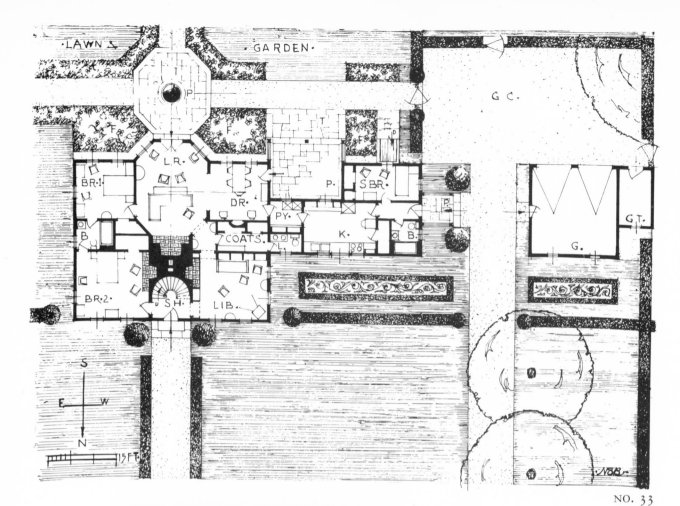

LAWN

GARDEN

G C.

S
E   W
N

15 FT

NO. 33

PERSPECTIVE

SECOND-FLOOR

EAST ELEVATION

NO. 34

THE WHITE-ELLERY HOUSE

Gloucester, Massachusetts   Original Built 1704

Drawing No. 33   This house was inspired by the "White-Ellery House" of Gloucester, Massachusetts. The house is a central-chimney lean-to type and is two and a half stories in height. The Second story overhangs the First floor and the end uprights are finished with carved terminals.

The Main unit contains an Entrance Hall with circular stairs to the Second Floor.

To the east are located two Bedrooms and Bath. Bedroom No. 2 has a fireplace. To the west of Stair Hall is located a Library which gives access to a large octagonal Living Room with a fireplace in both rooms. Off the Living Room is located a Coat Room and Dining Room. A one-story wing to the west provides a lavatory of the Coat Room, a Pantry, Kitchen, Servant's Bedroom and Bath. A large Porch with an entrance from Dining Room and Service Entry also gives access to a two-car Garage separated from the house as indicated.

Off the Living Room there is a large paved Terrace with a pool which gives access to lawn and garden areas.

Drawing No. 34   This drawing provides a Second Floor plan containing two large Bedrooms and Bath to the south and stairs to Attic rooms if so desired. Both Bedrooms have fireplaces.

This drawing also contains the east elevation and a perspective view of the house exterior taken from the east showing the landscaping.

The author introduced five windows on the Second Story, north front (indicated in floor plan), while the original house has only three.

Note: The back of the "White-Ellery House" as it now stands in Gloucester, faces north. The land around was known as the town green or common where stood the early church or meeting house, so history informs us.

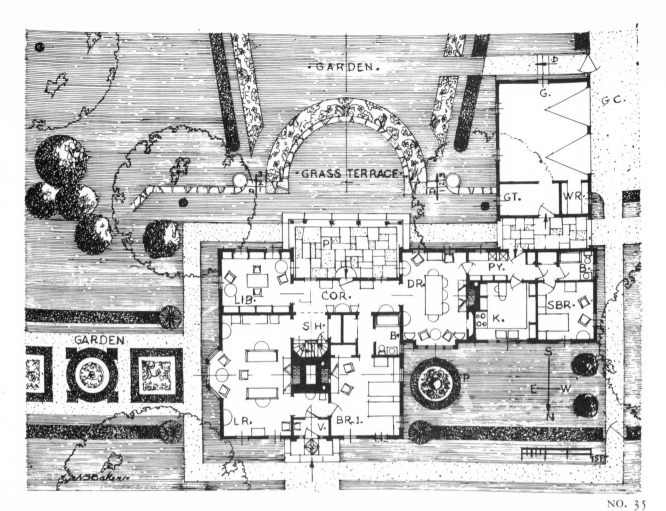

GARDEN.

GRASS TERRACE.

GARDEN

LIB.

COR.

DR.

P.

PY.

SH.

K.

B.

SBR.

LR.

V.

BR·1.

P.

GT.

WR.

G.

G.C.

D.

B.

S
E
W
N

NO. 35

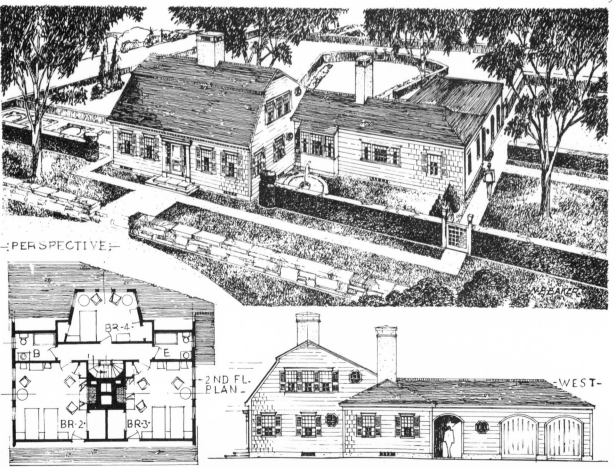

PERSPECTIVE

BR·4·

B

E

BR·2·

BR·3·

2ND FL.
PLAN·

WEST

NO. 36

THE ROBINSON HOUSE

Lanesville, Massachusetts   Original Built 1710

Drawing No. 35   The "Old Robinson House" of Lanesville, Massachusetts, inspired the house covered by the next two drawings. The house is composed of a Main Unit about square and is a central-chimney and gambrel-roof type. It is one-and-a-half stories high and has a one-story addition to the right of the Main Unit. It is a shingled house but whether it was originally, the author does not know.

On Drawing No. 35, the author has faced the house to the north on a beautiful stretch of countryside sloping to the south. The garden to the south is several steps below the Porch as indicated. It is viewed from the Living Room and from Bedroom No. 1 and the Dining Room.

The house is entered from a private road through a Vestibule Entrance. To the east there is a Living Room with bay window and fireplace. At the southerly end a Stair Hall is entered from a corridor in back of a long southerly Porch. At the east end of the corridor there is a Library. At the west end there is a Dining Room. There are coat closets and Bath and Toilet combination for the First Floor; also for Bedroom No. 1 which is on the northwest corner of the Main Unit. The Bedroom has a fireplace.

The westerly one-story extension contains a large Dining Room with bay window and fireplace. The remainder of the extension contains a combination Pantry and Laundry, a Kitchen, and Servant's Bedroom and Bath. The west extension turns at right angle to the south and contains a covered way which gives access to Kitchen and Main Garden. There is a two-car Garage and Garage court yard.

Drawing No. 36   This drawing contains a Second Floor Plan with three Bedrooms, two Bathrooms, and Stair Hall. Bedrooms No. 2 and No. 3 have fireplaces.

This drawing also contains the west elevation and a perspective view of the house taken from the northwest and the landscape in general. Because of the slight difference in elevation of the ground, a stone wall has been introduced between the front lawn and the private road to the house; also between southerly Terrace and Garden.

The reader will notice that the roof from the front is unbroken by dormers; with a gambrel roof, this house is very attractive.

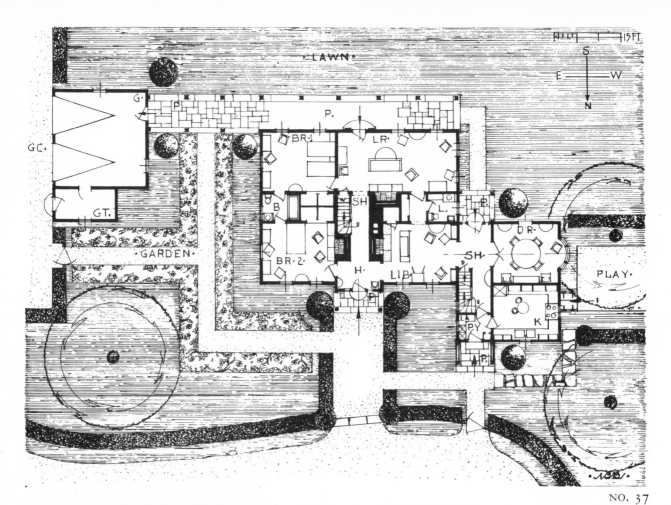

·LAWN·

S
E — W
N

GC·

G·
P
P·
BR·1
LR·
GT·
B
SH
L·
DR·
PLAY·
GARDEN·
BR·2
H·
LIB·
SH·
PY·
K
P·
P·

·NO. 37·

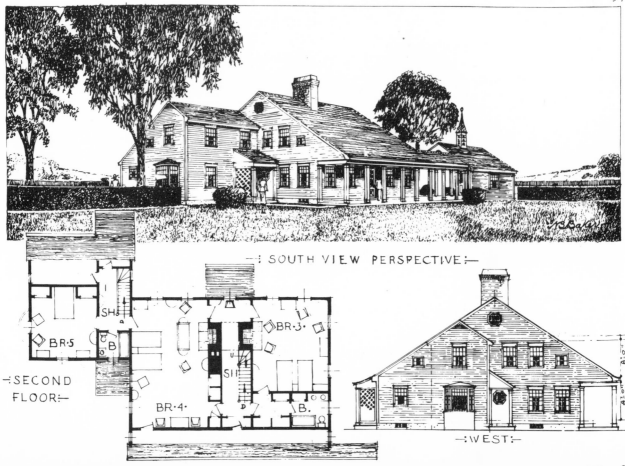

·SOUTH VIEW PERSPECTIVE·

SH·
BR·5
B·
BR·3
SH·
·SECOND FLOOR·
BR·4
B·

·WEST·

·NO. 38·

THE HAMMOND HOUSE

Eastville, New York   Original Built 1719

Drawing No. 37 "The Hammond House" in Eastville, New York, near Scarsdale, is the inspiration for this house covered by the author in drawings No. 37 to No. 39, inclusive. The landscape perspective indicates a site similar to the one the original house was built on—mainly open country with fields to the south and hilly country to the north, a wonderful site for a house of this type, large and rambling.

From a private road the house is entered from a simple Porch and the Stair Hall to the Living Room on the south side. Off the Stair Hall to the east is Bedroom No. 2 with fireplace, and off the Living Room to the east one enters Bedroom No. 1. A combination Bathroom for the Bedrooms is indicated. Off the Hall to the west there is a Library with fireplace and through a Passage with Lavatory and Coat Closet, the Living Room is entered again where a fireplace is provided. A Porch is carried across the south side of the house and connects with a Garage for two cars with accessories and a large court connected with the private drive to the house.

To the west is a Dining Room and Kitchen wing with north and south entrance, Porches and Stair Hall extending to the Second Floor above.

The Dining Room is provided with a bay window overlooking a Play Yard for the children. The Play Yard space can be used as a Garden.

Drawing No. 38 The Second Floor of the Main Unit contains two large Bedrooms and one Bathroom and each room is provided with a fireplace. The westerly wing contains one Bedroom and Bathroom, a Storage Room and Stair Hall to the First Floor.

This drawing, in addition to the Second Floor, contains a west elevation and a perspective view of the south of the house taken from the southwest and showing the long Porch and connection with Garage.

=FRONT VIEW PERSPECTIVE=
=NORTH=

Drawing No. 39   This drawing is another perspective view of the house taken from the front and road to same, showing the house drawn from the northeast.

    The Garden shows a narrow planting strip following each side of the path to the east of the house which is boxed in on the north side by a clipped hedge as indicated.

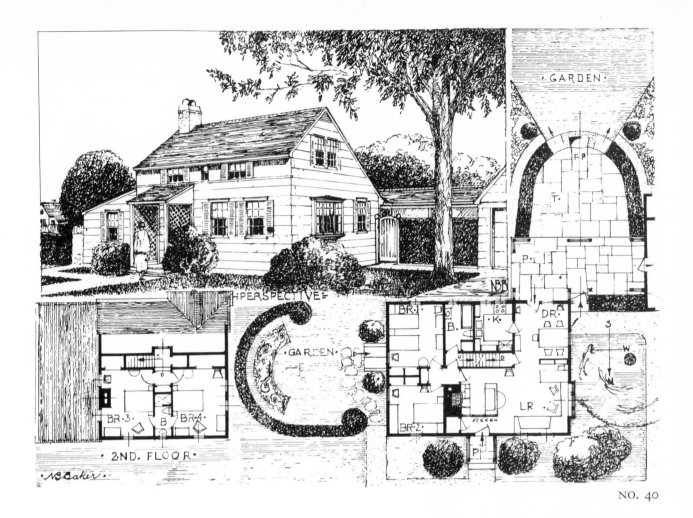

NO. 40

SMALL GABLE LEAN-TO

Wilton, Connecticut   Original Built 1725

Drawing No. 40   The inspiration for this house is a small "Gable Lean-to" in the town of Wilton, Connecticut. The house has been there a long time. The author has enlarged it slightly. The owner is not known; it opens every spring into an antique shop.

Forgetting for a while that the house is an antique shop and picturing what a fine small house could be made of it, the author arranged the First Floor plan to have two Bedrooms and Bath to the east, a Living Room and fireplace with a screened Entrance as shown, and a Dining Room and large Porch. A Terrace with a fireplace for outdoor cooking is shown, and a Garden and two-car Garage may be entered from the Porch.

A Kitchen, small but compact, and stairs to the Second Floor and Basement completes the First Floor plan.

The Second Floor plan contains two Bedrooms with a Bathroom with shower in between.

On the same drawing there is a perspective of the exterior of the house taken from the northwest and showing the solid background of planting, also the Garage and connecting Porch and landscaping.

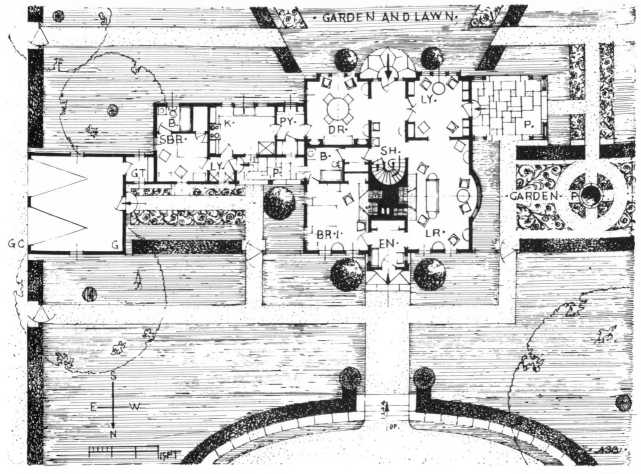

ᴛHE DENNISON HOUSE

Annisquam, Massachusetts   Original Built 1727

Drawing No. 41   This house of ancient vintage according to American standards is the result of an inspiration by "The Dennison Home" on Sandy Road, Annisquam, Massachusetts. The reader is referred to Drawing No. 42, the perspective of the house for the changes made in its outward appearance; changes made by the author which he believes makes for its improvement.

Drawing No. 41 is the First Floor Plan and its location on the property and some of the landscaping is shown.

Entering to the right or west side of the Stair Hall is a spacious Living Room with a large bay window and fireplace. To the southeast is the Dining Room and to the west the Library, thence to a large Porch to the west. On the east side of the house is a one-story Wing containing a Pantry and Kitchen, a Porch and Service Entrance; also a Servant's Room and Bath and

-: PERSPECTIVE :-

-: SECOND FLOOR :-

S H

BR·2·   B·   BR·3·

NO. 42

access to a two-car Garage and Garage court. To the east of the Entrance Hall is located a Guest Bedroom and Bath, the Bedroom having a fireplace.

In the landscaping, provision has been made for a large decorative hedge-enclosed garden extending east and west.

An Entrance Road on the north side is bordered by stone walls approaching the house to take care of the difference in grade, the ground around the house being several steps higher than the Entrance Road. Behind the wall is a low clipped hedge. Coping and steps of cut stone laid with uniform cement joints are shown. This applies to the Porch copings and pavement as well as to all terraces and steps.

Drawing No. 42   This drawing contains a perspective of the exterior taken from the north-west, and a Second Floor plan containing two large Bedrooms with fireplaces and connecting Bathroom to the north. A Stair Hall with Sitting area is on the south.

The changes in the perspective mentioned at the beginning were made by the author. The plan, section, and elevations of the Dennison house are of wonderful proportions and deserve a better treatment. The original building, the author is sure, was finished with narrow siding. A flush-boarded frieze has been added and is the height of the windows of the Second Floor on the north side.

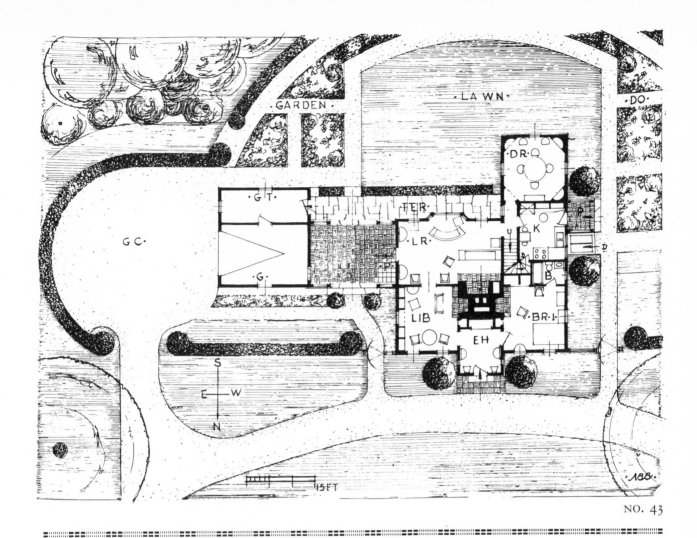

THE MARTIN HOUSE

Swansea, Cape Cod, Massachusetts   Original Built 1728

Drawing No. 43   The inspiration for this house is "The Martin House" of Swansea, Cape Cod, Massachusetts, and as one can see from the perspective it is a gambrel-roof house with a single chimney and three dormer windows on the front. If one goes through the pictures of old houses of this type, it is very unusual to find three dormers in the front. The roof of this type of house is almost invariably without dormers on the front. However, history tells us that the original house was burned by the Indians and the present building was rebuilt in 1728.

The First Floor plan features an Entrance Hall as one comes in from a private drive. Off this Hall one enters the Library from the east and from the Library the large Living Room is entered overlooking the Garden and wooded area. From the Living Room one enters a small area with Stairs to

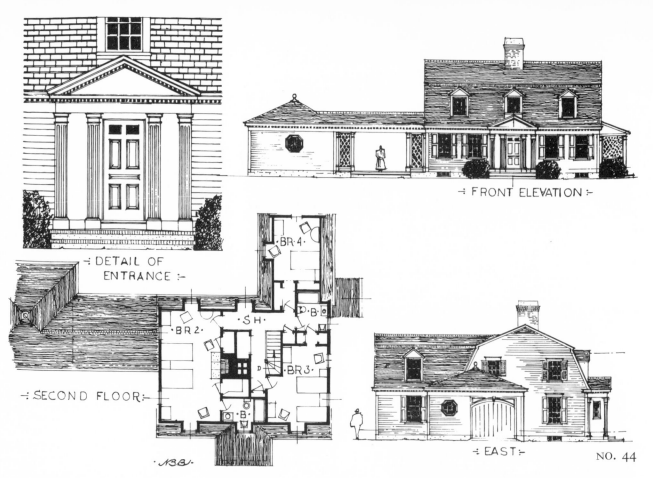

-: FRONT ELEVATION :-

-: DETAIL OF
ENTRANCE :-

-: SECOND FLOOR :-

·BR·4·

·B·

·S·H·

·BR·2·

·D·

·BR·3·

·B·

·NBC·

-: EAST :-

NO. 44

·PERSPECTIVE·

NO. 45

the Second Floor and where the Dining Room and Kitchen are located. The Dining Room overlooks the Garden and the Kitchen has a small outside Porch. Off the Entrance Hall to the west is a Guest Bedroom and Bath. The Bedroom, Library, and Living Room are provided with fireplaces.

To the east the author has provided a One-Story Addition thus arranging an outside Porch with entrance to the Living Room and Terrace overlooking the Garden. There is also a connecting Garage, Garage Court, and accessories.

Drawing No. 44   This drawing contains a plan of the Second Floor including a Stair Hall, three Bedrooms, and two Bathrooms.

The drawing also includes a Front elevation, east elevation, and a detail of the Main Entrance all drawn to scale.

Drawing No. 45   This entire drawing is given over to a perspective view of the house taken from the northwest and indicating the Garden, landscaping, and surrounding countryside as imagined by the author: A compact house on plenty of land with woodland and scenery all around. On the whole, a most enjoyable place.

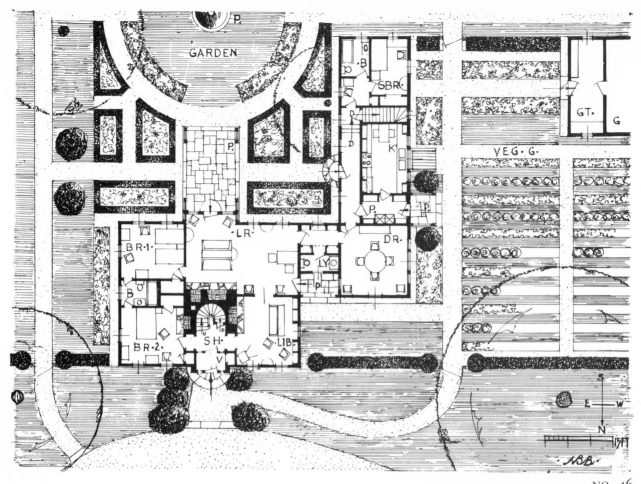

GARDEN

SBR.

K

VEG·G·

GT. G

LR·

BR·1·

DR·

B

LY

P

BR·2· SH· LIB

S
E — W
N

15 FT

·NBB·

NO. 46

-PERSPECTIVE-

BR·3· BR·4·

·2ND·FLOOR·

SH·

NO. 47

THE HALLETT-THATCHER HOUSE

Yarmouth, Massachusetts　　　　　Original Built 1730

Drawing No. 46　　This house is a one-chimney, one-and-one-half-story Cape Cod House with a gable roof and addition as indicated. It was inspired by the "Hallet-Thatcher House" at Yarmouth, Cape Cod, Massachusetts.

Many old Cape Cod Houses have been built and still exist but in many cases as families grew, the houses expanded beyond the length of the original ridge pole. Other ridge poles were added and rooms at different levels resulted the whole in a rather haphazard development. This house, however, has been studied and added to in a systematic and architectural manner.

The plan of the First Floor is as follows: From a private driveway one enters a Vestibule and then a Stair Hall with rounded windows at back of stairs. From the Stair Hall to the east are located Bedrooms No. 2 and No. 1 with Bathroom between. Bedroom No. 2 is provided with a fireplace. To the west from the Stair Hall one enters the Library and from this room the large Living Room. From the east end of the Living Room Bedroom No. 1 is entered and from the west end is located a Shower Room and Lavatory.

Through a Passage Way from the Living Room one enters the Dining Room and a one-story wing. This wing contains besides the Dining Room a Pantry, Kitchen and Kitchen Entrance porch. Here is also a stairway to the Basement and a Bedroom and Bath for Servants. A separate two-car Garage is reached from the Kitchen Entrance Porch.

Drawing No. 47　　This drawing contains the Second Floor plan with two large Bedrooms each with fireplace and Bathroom.

A perspective of the house with view taken from the northwest is also included on this drawing as indicated.

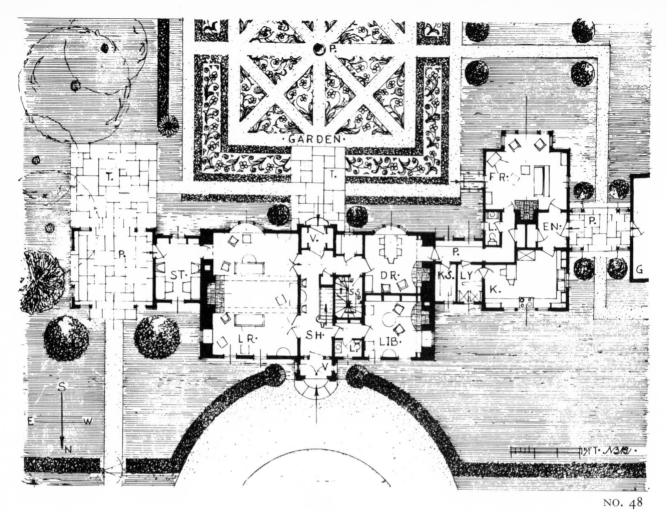

GARDEN

NO. 48

THE SHORT HOUSE

Newburg, Massachusetts   Original Built 1733

Drawing No. 48   There are not many of this type of Early American houses found today throughout New England. This house is of frame construction except the gable ends of the main unit which are constructed of brick or stone masonry so that the fireplaces and chimneys could be placed at each end of the house in any location desired by the occupants. The masonry ends were of heavy construction but were also tied to the wood framing of sides in an ingenious manner.

Before we go inside the house, let's take a quick walk around the grounds. One approaches the house by a private road to a circular hedged-in drive with lawn in the center. To the east a gate in the hedge leads you to a combination enclosed Porch and Terrace, also to a large square patterned garden. From here a walk leads to a Porch and Family Room and to the Service Wing with Garage and turn-around.

The inspiration for this house is "The Short House" located at Newburg, Massachusetts.

The First Floor plan is as follows: From the circular driveway one enters a Vestibule Entrance to Stair Hall running through the house. At the southerly end another Vestibule Entrance gives access to a large Terrace and the Garden. From the east side of the stair Hall double doors open to the Living Room which has a fireplace on the east wall and circular bay window on the south.

From the Living Room to the east is a study with desk and bookcases. The study opens on to a large enclosed Porch and Terrace. From the Stair Hall to the west a Lavatory is located on the north end. A Coat Closet is on the south end and between is located a staircase to Service Rooms on the second and third floors.

On the First Floor to the west one passes into the Library on the north side and to the Dining Room on the south side. Both of these rooms have fireplaces in the masonry wall.

From the Dining Room a one-story addition is provided. This includes a Passage-way with a Pantry leading to a Family Room with fireplace and large bay window which overlooks the Garden. The remainder of the Wing includes a Lavatory, Kitchen, Store Room, and Service Entrance. A Porch connects to a two-car Garage.

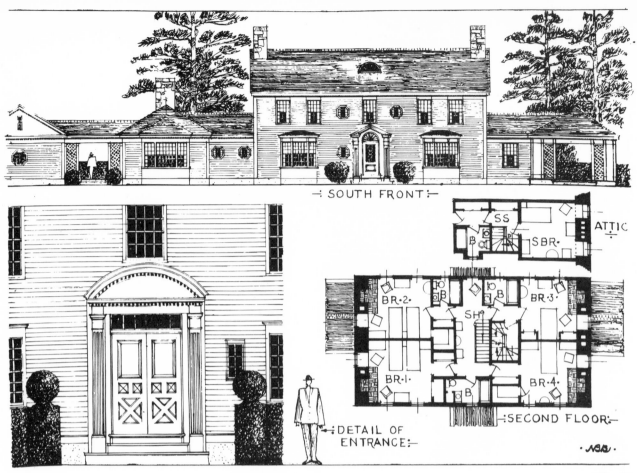

—: SOUTH FRONT :—

ATTIC

SS

SBR·

B

BR·2·

B

B

SH⁰

BR·3·

B

BR·1·

B

BR·4·

—: SECOND FLOOR :—

·ᴬᴮᴮ·

—: DETAIL OF ENTRANCE :—

NO. 49

Drawing No. 49 This drawing includes the plan of the Second Floor, the Servant's Bedroom on the Third Floor, a drawing of the south Front, and a scale detail of the north Front Entrance.

The Second Floor plan includes four Bedrooms with fireplaces provided in the masonry gable end walls. Three Bathrooms, ample closet space, and a Servant's Room with service Stair Hall are as indicated.

The Third Floor provides additional Service Bedrooms and Bath. The remainder of the Attic or Third Floor can be used for storage.

A full-height Basement is provided under the Main Unit and Service Wing.

PERSPECTIVE

NO. 50

Drawing No. 50   This drawing provides a perspective of the entire building. The view is taken from the northeast showing the appearance of the house as it is approached from the north. The site is as drawn and imagined by the author.

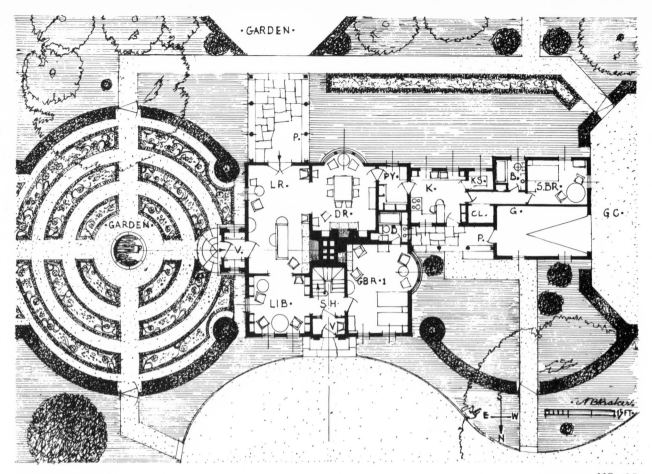

· GARDEN ·

· GARDEN ·

NO. 51

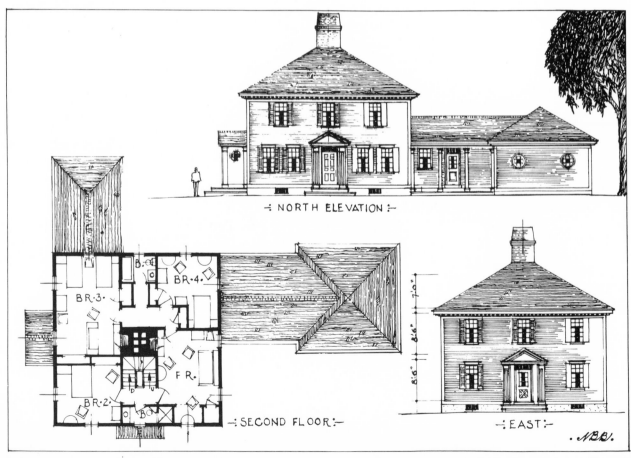

· NORTH ELEVATION ·

· SECOND FLOOR ·

· EAST ·

NO. 52

THE OLD COLLINS HOUSE

Gloucester, Massachusetts   Original Built 1740

Drawing No. 51   This is a very unusual house. The Main Unit is a square plan with a hip-roof which finishes against a 5-feet by 5-feet central brick chimney evenly on all four sides as indicated. The inspiration for it is "The Old Collins House" at Gloucester, Massachusetts, and the original house was built in 1740.

The main section of the First Floor Plan is composed on the east side of a Library and Living Room and a large Porch to the south. This section of the house overlooks a circular Garden of considerable size enclosed in a clipped hedge. The house is entered through a Vestibule as indicated. A Garden such as this takes considerable time and patience to care for and there are simpler schemes for the space if so desired, but it is certainly worth the effort to carry it out, as it is decorative in summer as well as in winter.

The First Floor is entered by Vestibule from a private road on the north side of the house. Inside is the Stair Hall on the west side of which is the large Guest Bedroom No. 1 and Bath. This room has a bay window and a fireplace. The Living Room adjoins the Dining Room on the south side of the house. Both rooms have fireplaces. A Pantry serves the Dining Room.

A one-story, hip-roofed addition has been added to the west of the Main Unit and it contains a Kitchen, Porch, Store Closet, and Servant's Bedroom and Bath. A one-car Garage and separate garden tool house are off to one side of the Court. If the owner does not require Servant's quarters, the space can be turned over to the Garage making it a two-car capacity in place of one.

Drawing No. 52   This drawing contains a Second Floor Plan showing Bedrooms No. 2 and No. 3 to the east of a Family Room and Bedroom No. 4 to the west. Also, two Bathrooms and a Stair Hall are shown, as well as Bedroom No. 3 and Family Room which contain fireplaces.

This drawing shows the north exterior elevation and the east or Garden elevation, each drawn to scale.

NO. 53

Drawing No. 53   This drawing is a perspective of the exterior of the house taken from the northeast. It includes the landscaping and site which, of course, shows the round Garden to the east, the southerly Lawn, roads, and Garage Court.

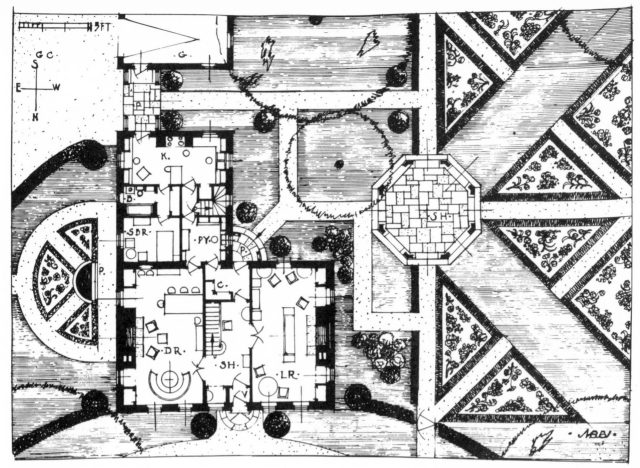

THE VAN DEUSEN HOUSE

Hurley, New York   Original Built 1744

Drawing No. 54   "The Van Deusen House" located in the town of Hurley, New York, on the bank of the Hudson River, is the inspiration for this house covered by the author's drawings.

It is built of stone most beautifully laid in the year 1744 and according to historical accounts was the temporary State Capitol in 1777. The author's branch of the Van Deusen family settled in the town of Kinderhook across the Hudson River where his mother, Orietta Van Deusen, married Norman B. Baker, Sr., in 1881.

The house as planned by the author has a first floor arrangement featuring a central Stair Hall with a Coat Room at the south end where it opens on a Porch and path leading to a lattice summer house. On the east end of the Hall is a large Dining Room with fireplace and on the west side a Living

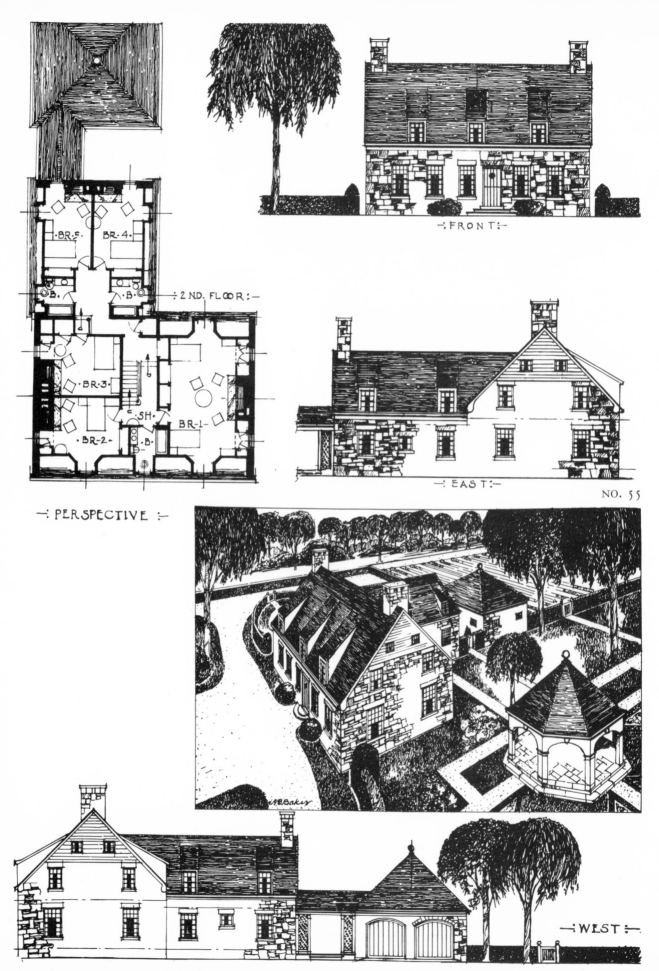

-: FRONT :-

-: 2 ND. FLOOR :-

·BR·5· ·BR·4·

·B· ·B·

·BR·3·

·SH· ·BR·1·

·BR·2· ·B·

-: PERSPECTIVE :-

-: EAST :-

NO. 55

-: WEST :-

NO. 56

Room the full width of the house also with fireplace. The southerly Wing contains a large Kitchen, Pantry, Stairs to Basement, and Servant's Bedroom and Bath. At the southeast end of the Kitchen a covered Porch leads to a two-car Garage.

Drawing No. 55   This drawing contains the Second Floor Plan the Front and east elevations drawn to scale.

The Second Floor of the Main Wing contains three Bedrooms with fireplaces as indicated; also a Stair Hall. The rear Wing is at a slightly lower level and this space contains the Bedrooms and Baths as indicated.

The Front and east elevations with their high sixteen-light windows and long, roof-dormers are reminiscent of Hudson River Dutch.

Drawing No. 56   This drawing contains the west elevation drawn to scale with Garage, a building unheard of in those days and a perspective of the house drawn from the northwest which features the Summer House. Few houses had porches in those days.

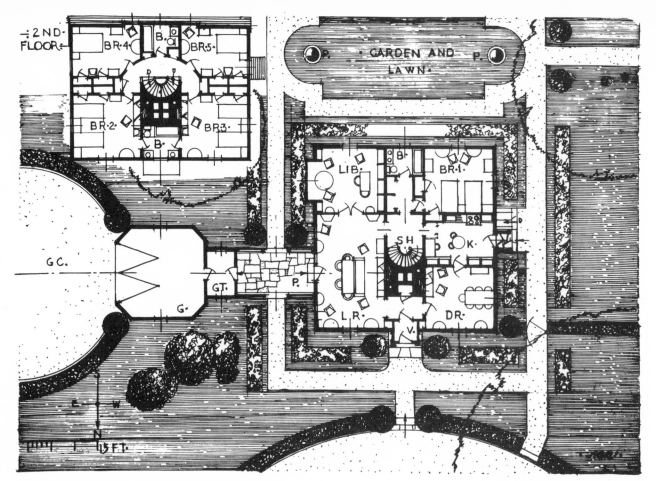

2ND FLOOR

BR·4 B. & D BR·5.

BR·2. B. BR·3.

GARDEN AND LAWN.

P. P.

LIB. B. BR·1.

SH K.

GC. GT. P.

G. L.R. DR.

V.

E — W

N 45 F.T.

NO. 57

:·PERSPECTIVE·:

7'·0"

7'·6"

8'·6"

:·NORTH ELEVATION·: :·WEST·:

NO. 58

THE OLD GRISWOLD HOUSE

Guilford, Connecticut   Original Built 1750

Drawing No. 57 The old house that inspired the house on this drawing is the "Old Gris-wold House" on Post Road in Guilford, Connecticut. As a person passes by in a car, the house stands out like a faultless gem.

While Guilford stands out as a village of many historic houses, this one, to the author, is especially fine.

The First Floor Plan is as follows: Through a Vestibule Entrance to the east is a Living Room and Library and long Porch, also a Garage and Court.

To the right is a Dining Room, Kitchen, and Porch. To the south is a Bedroom and Bath with circular stairs in Stair Hall to the Second Floor and Basement.

On the same drawing is located the Second Floor Plan composed of two Bedrooms with fireplaces and baths as indicated. Also shown are two Bed-rooms with Bath between on the south side as well as half-circular stairs in the Stair Hall.

Drawing No. 58 On this drawing is located a front or north elevation, a west elevation and a perspective view of the house and grounds taken from the northwest side as indicated.

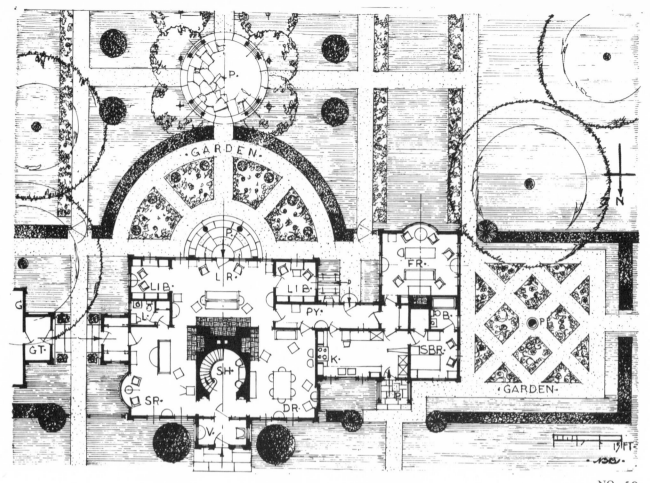

GARDEN

P.

LIB.   L.R.   LIB.   FR.

PY.   B.

G.   SBR.

GT.   K.   GARDEN   P.

SR.   SH.   DR.

V.   P.

15 FT.

NO. 59

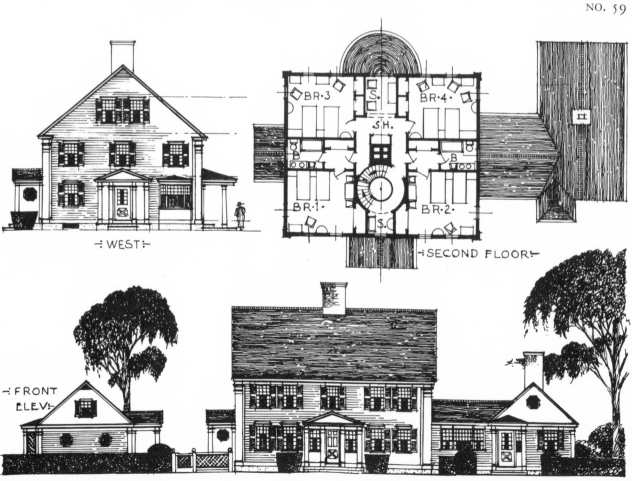

BR·3   S.   BR·4

SH.

B.   B.

BR·1   BR·2

S.

WEST   SECOND FLOOR

FRONT
ELEV.

NO. 60

THE LAURA HOOPER HOUSE

New Ipswich, New Hampshire　　　Original Built 1752

Drawing No. 59　　This house is inspired by the "Laura Hooper House" located in New Ipswich, New Hampshire. It is a fairly large, single house. This drawing is the First Floor plan, composed by the author as follows: From a private road, the house is entered through a Vestibule which gives access to a circular Stair Hall with stairs to the Second Floor. Through an arched opening to the east, a Family Room is entered and to the west, a Dining Room through a similar arched opening. Adjoining the Living Room is a small Library. All three rooms have fireplaces. To the south of the Living Room one enters a semi-circular Porch beyond which are two small Gardens with a circular Summer House between. On the east from the Family Room is a Vestibule with Coat Closets. A few feet beyond the house is a two-car Garage. Through a passage-way is a one-story addition including a Kitchen and Porch, a corridor to the Children's Playroom with a fireplace, and a Servant's Bedroom and Bath.

Drawing No. 60　　This drawing contains a plan of the Second Floor and front and west elevations.

　　The Second Floor Plan contains four Bedrooms and two Bathrooms and, of course, the circular stairs from the First Floor extending to the Third Floor or Attic where two rooms can be added.

= PERSPECTIVE =

NO. 61

Drawing No. 61   This drawing is a perspective of the exterior of the house taken from the northwest indicating the landscaping of the property.

    The details of the Entrance Vestibule and the four corners of the Main Unit are outstanding, decorative features.

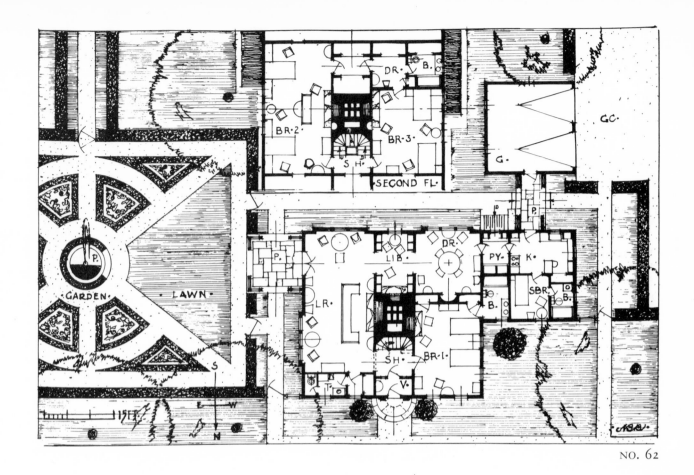

THE ATWOOD HOUSE

Chatham, Massachusetts   Original Built 1752

Drawing No. 62   This is the layout of the First and Second Floors of a Cape Cod gambrel-roof house and the inspiration for it is "The Atwood House" of Chatham, Massachusetts, on the Cape. This is a typical and most satisfying house of its type on the Cape. It was built in the year 1752 by Joseph Atwood, a navigator of parts of the world unknown at that time. There was a long line of families of the Atwood name and the house has been taken over and maintained by the Chatham Historical Society.

The First Floor consists of a Vestibule Entrance and Stair Hall to the Second Floor. To the east is a large Living Room leading to a small Library with fireplace and beyond is the Dining Room. A Porch overlooks a square, hedged-in Garden, as indicated. On the west side of Stair Hall is a Guest or Main Bedroom and Bath.

-: PERSPECTIVE :-

-: EAST :-

-: FRONT-VIEW :-

NO. 63

From the Stair Hall to the west is a large Bedroom with Bath and fireplace. To the west the author has also added a one-story addition or wing containing Kitchen and Pantry, Servant's Bedroom and Bath. To the south there is also a Covered Way as combination Service Entrance and a two-car Garage. There is a large Garage Court and private road to the house.

The Second Floor Plan in this drawing contains two large Bedrooms, Bathroom, and Stair Hall. There are fireplaces for all rooms where so indicated.

Drawing No. 63   This drawing includes front and west elevations drawn to scale and a perspective drawing of the exterior taken from a northwesterly point and indicating the house on the property and the landscaping.

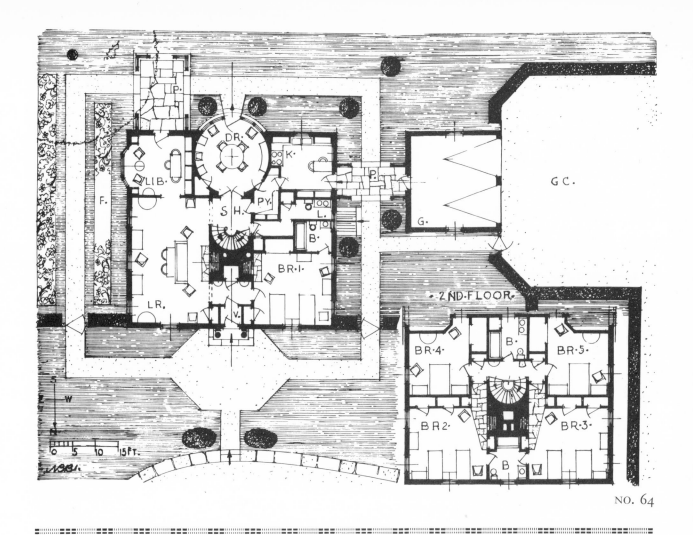

THE JOSEPH DAY HOUSE

W. Springfield, Massachusetts   Original Built 1754

Drawing No. 64   This drawing contains both the First and Second Floor Plans of the house which was inspired by the brick-walled "Joseph Day House," a salt-box type built in 1754.

According to history, it is one of the rare "salt-boxes" to be built of brick and it is owned and operated by the Ramapogue Historical Society. It is a beautiful building and the author hopes he has done it justice in his perspective. The house has a very broad brick chimney.

The plan is the author's and he has added a good-sized Porch on the southeast corner and a one-story addition to the west creating a Service Porch and connecting Entrance to a two-car Garage.

What bond was used in laying up the brick of this house, the author does not know, but the brick can be laid up in common, English, Flemish, or

Dutch Bond as the owner may select. For colonial houses the brick should be red in color.

The First Floor Plan features an Entrance Vestibule from a private road. To the east one enters a large Living Room with a fireplace. At the southerly end of the Living Room is a Library and from the Library an outside Porch as indicated. Off the southerly end of the Living Room is a Stair Hall with circular stairs. Adjoining this is a circular Dining Room which has a large glazed southerly exposure with doors to the outside.

Off the Dining Room is a Pantry leading to Stair Hall and a Kitchen to the west. The Kitchen has a Porch connecting to a two-car Garage with a good-size, paved Garage court. Off the Entrance Hall on the north front is located a Guest Bedroom No. 1 with Bath and fireplace. A First Floor Lavatory is located on the west side of the Stair Hall back of the Pantry.

The Second Floor, also indicated on this drawing, consists of two Bedrooms with fireplaces and connecting Bathroom on the north front, two Bedrooms and Bath, and Stair Hall with circular stairs on the southerly side of the house.

Drawing No. 65   This drawing contains a perspective with view taken from the northeast and indicating the development of the property.

The location of the property and type, and landscaping is imagined by the author.

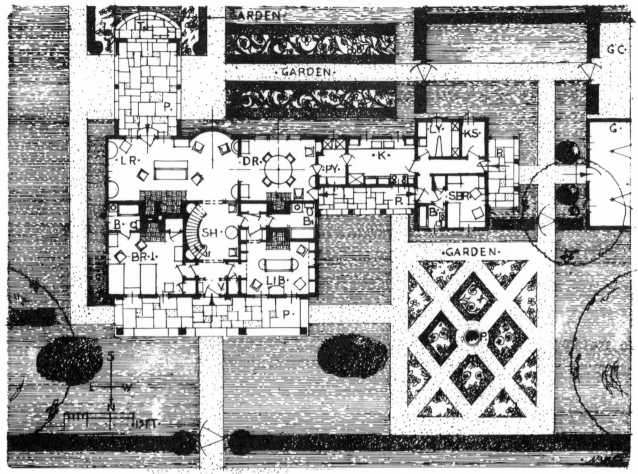

THE HENRY HOUSE

N. Bennington, Vermont   Original Built 1769

Drawing No. 66   This is a drawing of the First Floor Plan and its relation to the property on which it sits. The Main Unit has a two-story gable-roof and a two-story Porch the length of the Main Unit, formed by four square posts and added onto the ridge-roof as indicated. As the main Garden is on the south side of the house, the livable Porch of the Living Room is on this side. The author has added a one-story Service Wing to the west side of the Main Unit. The Porch with its square columns is the type one expects to find in the south, not in a state like Vermont.

The inspiration for this house is "The Henry House" of North Bennington, Vermont.

The plan of the First Floor is as follows: From a private road one enters the two-story Porch with a Vestibule Entrance to a Main Passage. Bedroom

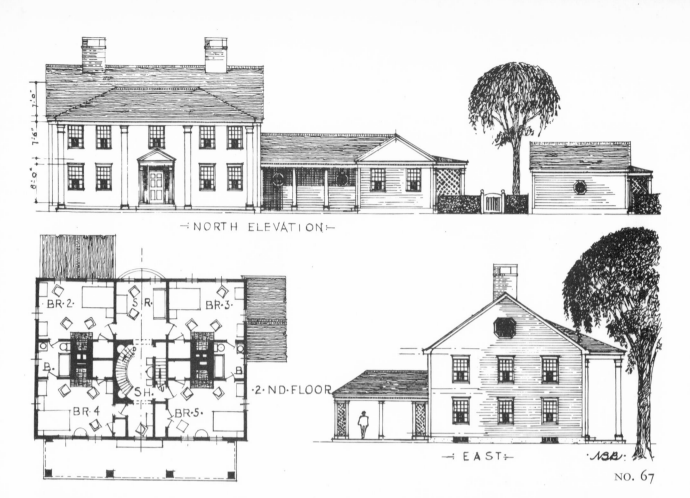

=NORTH ELEVATION=

·S·R·

BR·2·

BR·3·

B·

B·

·2·ND·FLOOR·

·SH·

BR·4·

BR·5·

=EAST=

NO. 67

=PERSPECTIVE=

NO. 68

No. 1 is on the east with Bathroom and fireplace and to the west is a comfortable Library with a fireplace. South of this room is coat space and Lavatory. From the passage way mentioned one enters a large, curved Stair Hall which leads to the Living Room and the Dining Room on the south side of the Main Unit and to the Second Floor.

The one-story addition to the west added by the author, contains a Pantry, Kitchen, and Porch giving access to the Dining Room and Kitchen. A Servant's Room and Bath, Laundry, Kitchen Stores, and Service Porch are also in the Wing. A two-car Garage and large Garage Court are shown.

Decorated Gardens and clipped hedges are as indicated.

Drawing No. 67   This drawing contains a scale drawing of the north elevation of the entire house and Garage. The Finished boarding is flush finished where it is not indicated as bevelled siding.
This drawing shows the east Elevation and south and north Porches.

The Second Floor plan is shown providing four Bedrooms all with fireplaces and connecting Baths, a Stair Hall and separate stairs to the Attic where a room at either end can be provided if needed and Sitting Spaces off Halls where indicated.

Drawing No. 68   This drawing is a perspective view of the entire group, main house, wing, and separate garage.

The water scene is imaginary. The clipped hedges accent the gardens both north and south.

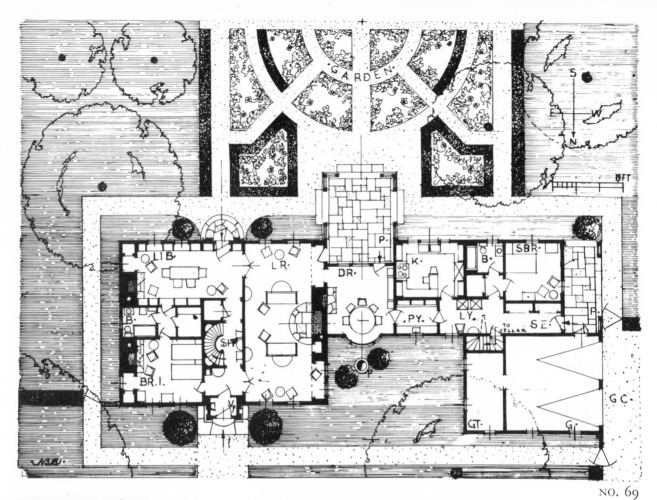

GARDEN

LIB. LR. DR. P. K. SBR. B.

B. PY. LY. SE. P.

BR.I. SH. TO CELLAR

GT. G. GC.

NO. 69

— PERSPECTIVE —

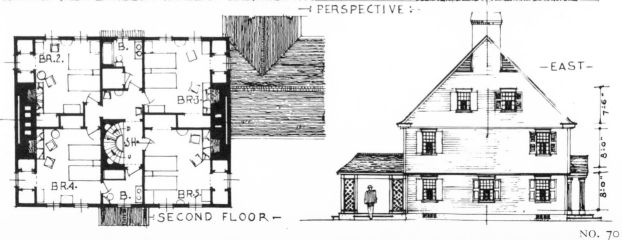

BR.2. B.

BR.3.

SH.

BR.4. B. BR.5.

— SECOND FLOOR —

— EAST —

NO. 70

THE MESSENGER HOUSE

Harwinton, Connecticut   Original Built 1783

Drawing No. 69

This is a drawing of a stately house. "The Messenger House," in the town of Harwinton, Connecticut. A one-story Wing has been added on the west side to bring the house up to date and make it much more livable.

The First Floor, as laid out, has a long Porch provided on the south side of the one-story addition with access both from the long Living Room and the Dining Room. From these rooms and Porch, a Garden can be seen and it is a feature with possibilities of unlimited beauty if planted properly.

The Main Unit of the house on the First Floor has a Vestibule Entrance and to the left or east is Bedroom No. 1 and Bath, the Bath serving also as the main First Story Lavatory. To the south on the east side of the hall is a large Library—both this room and Bedroom No. 1 have fireplaces. To the west side of the Stair Hall is located the Living Room, the full width of the unit as indicated. This room is also provided with a fireplace.

To the west of the Living Room one enters the Dining Room in the one-story addition. In this wing also are located the Pantry and Kitchen, Laundry, Service Entrance and Porch, the Servant's Bedroom and Bath. To the north of this Wing is a stair to the Basement, a two-car Garage, and Garage Court.

Drawing No. 70

This drawing contains the Second Floor Plan showing four Bedrooms with fireplaces for each and two Bathrooms. A Stair Hall leads to the First Floor and to a large Attic which can provide two more Rooms and Bath if so desired, as well as ample storage space.

This drawing also shows the east elevation and a perspective view of the entire house. It is to be noted that this is a woodframe building with two chimney stacks of brick and adaptable so that fireplaces can be placed in all main rooms of the Main Unit.

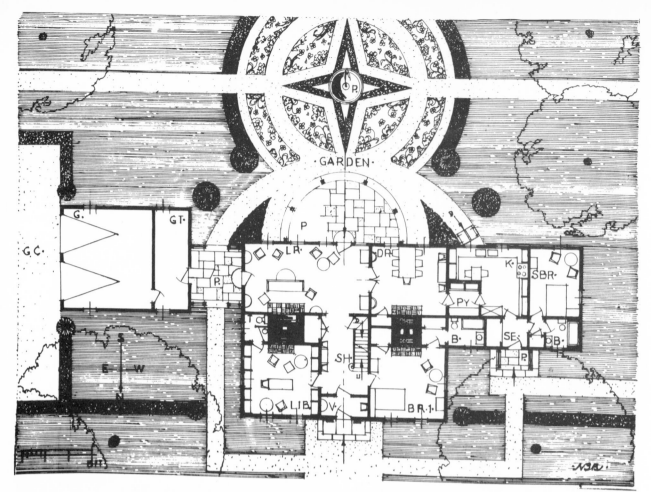

GARDEN

G. · GT·

GC·

P·

LR· DR· K· SBR·

PY·

B· SE· B·

P·

SH·

LIB· V· BR·1·

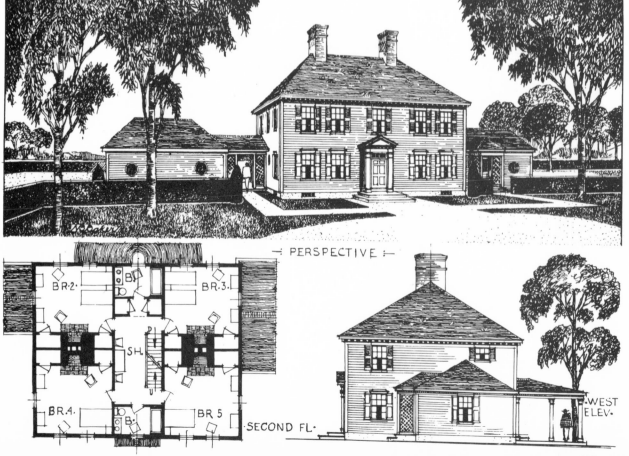

= PERSPECTIVE =

BR·2· BR·3·

SH·

BR·4· BR 5·

SECOND FL·

WEST ELEV·

THE COL. MEANS HOUSE

Amherst, New Hampshire   Original Built 1685

Drawing No. 71   This house was inspired by "The Colonel Means House" of Amherst, New Hampshire. The house has a hipped-roof with chimney back from each end on ridge line as indicated. Each principal room in the main section of the house has a fireplace. One enters a Vestibule Entrance (road not shown) connecting with Garage Court. From the Vestibule one enters the Stair Hall where stairs go from Cellar to Attic and the Hall extends to the Living Room on the east and Dining Room on the west. On the south side of Living Room there is a half-round, paved, covered Porch overlooking a circular Garden with Pool of interesting design. From the Living Room to the east is a small Porch which connects with a Garden Tool Room and a two-car Garage with a large Garage Court. Off the Stair Hall to the east is a Library and Lavatory. To the west, Bedroom No. 1 and Bath are both on the north and Entrance side of the house. To the right or west side of Main Unit a one-story Wing connects with the Main Unit and contains a Pantry and Kitchen, Service Entry and Servant's Bedroom and Bath.

Clipped hedges outline all portions of the exterior layout. A star-shaped fountain and pool in the center of circular Garden provides an interesting feature.

Drawing No. 72   This drawing shows a Second Floor Plan containing four Bedrooms and two Baths and Stair Hall.

This drawing also shows the west elevation with its hipped-roof showing and a perspective of the exterior with its two chimneys, the landscaping, and property from the northeast view.

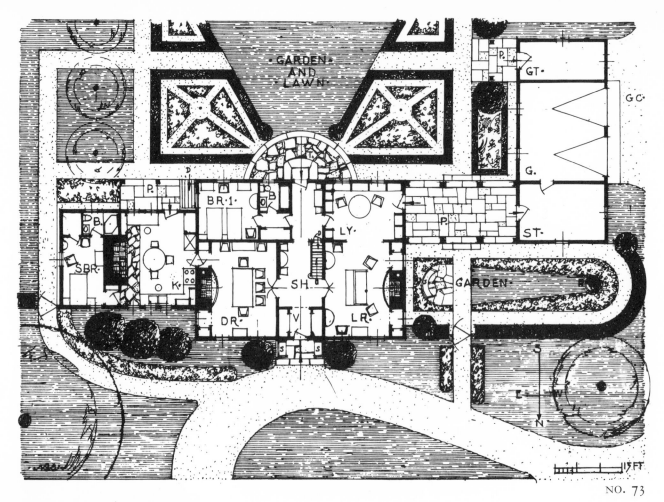

· GARDEN · AND · LAWN ·

P. A.
GT.
G C.
G.
ST.

D
P.
BR·1·
B
LY.
P.
GARDEN·
B
SBR·
K.
SH·
DR·
V
LR·
S S
15 FT

NO. 73

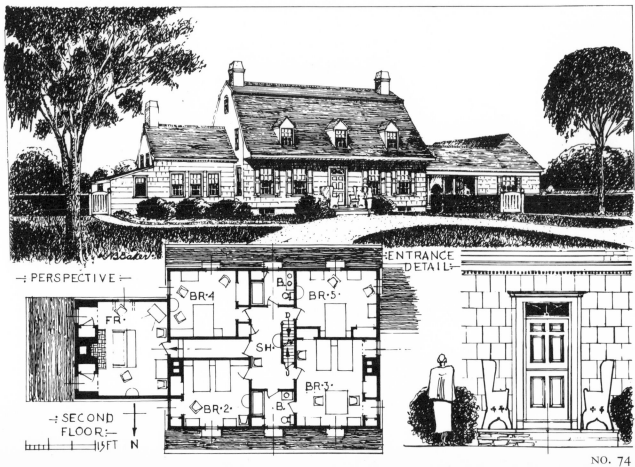

·Baker·

·PERSPECTIVE·

·ENTRANCE
DETAIL·

FR·

B
BR·4·
BR·5·
D
SH·

BR·2·
B.
BR·3·

·SECOND
FLOOR·
N
15 FT

NO. 74

THE VANDERVEER HOUSE

Flatbush, L.I., New York   Original Built 1787

Drawing No. 73 This house as planned and the perspective or exterior view is one the author believes to be one of the finest examples of the simple Dutch Domestic architecture in the state of New York. It was carefully measured among many other buildings by the author in the year 1919 and was taken apart and re-erected up-state by a prominent Great Neck, Long Island, builder named Richardson. The house when measured was in perfect condition both inside and out and was one of the finest examples of prefabrication the author has ever witnessed.

When one speaks of prefabrication it is never applied to houses hundreds of years old but with many of our early homes the frame was cut to proper size away from the site on which it was to be built and all the main joints were cut to size and housed and dowelled with oak or other hard wood dowels. Floor beams were nailed with hand wrought nails. It was not until years later that machine, wrought-iron nails were made.

The house described and used to inspire these drawings was "The Vandeveer House" in Flatbush, Long Island, New York. The house, before it was taken apart, stood diagonally across the intersection of two main roads in Flatbush which had to be extended.

The plan of the First Floor is as follows: From a private road, a Vestibule Entrance leads to a central Stair Hall and from this Hall to the right or west side is a Living Room with a fireplace and to the south of the Living Room, a Library. From the Library one enters a large Porch on the west elevation and Garage with accessories and large Garage Court. The Porch and Garage are located in a one-story Wing added by the author.

To the east, entered from the Stair Hall is the Dining Room with fireplace and Bedroom No. 1 with Bath. To the south of the Stair Hall is a paved Terrace overlooking a large hedged-in Garden and lawn. To the east is a two-story and lean-to Wing containing an old-fashioned Kitchen with large fireplace, with a Servant's Bedroom and Bath in the one-story section.

Drawing No. 74 This drawing contains a plan of the Second Floor with four Bedrooms and two Baths. A Passage leads from the Stair Hall to a Family Room with a fireplace in the easterly Wing.

On this drawing is also a detail of the simple Entrance used in these New York State Dutch houses and a perspective of the house complete in simple and beautiful form.

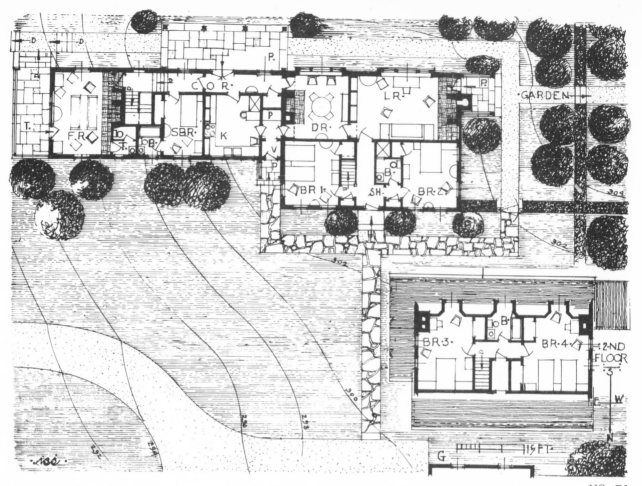

PERSPECTIVE

THE OLD BRICK HOUSE

Green Mountains, Vermont   Original Built 1790

Drawing No. 75   The original house which inspired these drawings, is in the foothills of the Green Mountains in Vermont. It is a mellow, old brick house which sits serenely along a hilltop with mountains all around.

   The author was the architect who remodeled the house. The First and Second Floor plans are shown on this drawing. The First Floor entrance faces north and the door opens directly to the Stair Hall which leads across the house to a large Living Room. Here is found an old fireplace with its original back-oven built into the wall. On the south, replacing a solid wall, is a long, shallow bay window filled with a superb view of the mountains. A Porch to the west of this room opens to a lovely informal Garden enclosed by a low wall of native stone. On the east side of the room is a wide doorway to the Dining Room which leads to a Porch and Terrace highwalled above the valley overlooking a panoramic view of the mountains.

   On the First Floor plan the Stair Hall shows a Bedroom and Bath on the west and a Bedroom on the east as well as the Stairway to the Second Floor where there are two Bedrooms and Bath.

   On the east side of the house the author has added a one-story Wing which steps downhill a short flight of stairs below the Main House and is entered through a corridor from the Dining Room. Off the corridor to the north is the Kitchen and Pantry; also a Servant's Bedroom and Bath. At the east end of the Wing is a Family or Sitting Area looking down on the valley from this vantage point.

Drawing No. 76   This drawing shows a perspective indicating how the house sits on top of a hill above the surrounding landscape.

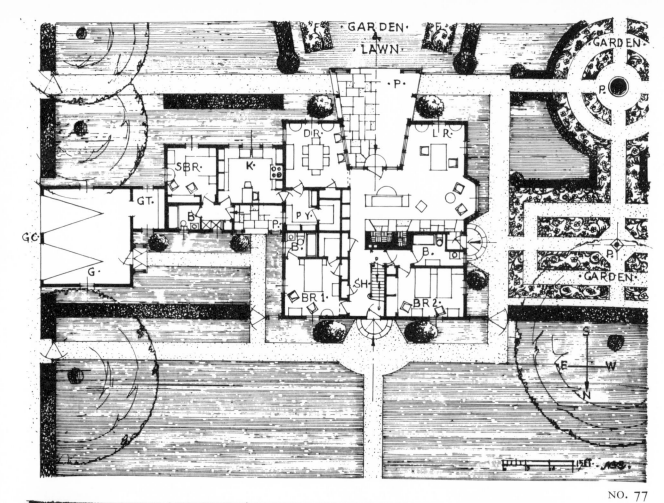

GARDEN
LAWN
GARDEN

P.

DIR.
L.R.

SBR.
K.

GT.

B.
P.
P.Y.
B.
B.

G.C.

G.
B.

SH.
BR 1.
BR 2.

GARDEN

P.

S
E
W
N

NO. 77

:SOUTH ELEVATION:

:EAST:

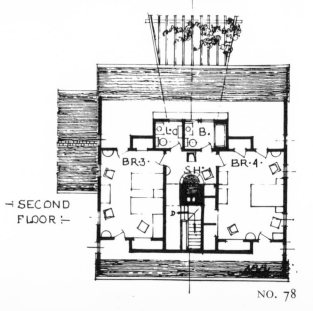

:SECOND
FLOOR:

B.
BR.3.
BR.4.
SH.

NO. 78

THE GILLIES HOUSE

Versailles, Connecticut   Original Built 1795

Drawing No. 77   From a path on a private road, one enters a Stair Hall shown on the First Floor plan. On each side, both east and west, is a Bedroom and Bath. Passing from the Stair Hall to the south, one enters a large Living Room with fireplace and to the right of the Living Room or east side is a Dining Room. Off the Living and Dining Rooms on this side of the house is a large tapered Porch half recessed under the house roof and half beyond the building line. The Porch, Living and Dining Rooms and west Bedroom overlook Gardens and lawns, where a west entrance is provided to the Living Room.

To the east is a one-story addition made by the author to provide a Kitchen Service Porch, a Servant's Bedroom and Bath as well as a two-car Garage and Garage Court.

This house is inspired by a single-chimney, gambrel-roof house in the outskirts of a town called Versailles above Norwich, Connecticut. The house was built about 1795.

Drawing No. 78   This drawing contains a Second Floor plan with two Bedrooms, Bath, Lavatory and Stair Hall with fireplace. It also contains a south and east elevation drawn to scale.

-: PERSPECTIVE :-

NO. 79

Drawing No. 79   This drawing contains a perspective view of the house from point indicated, and landscaping.

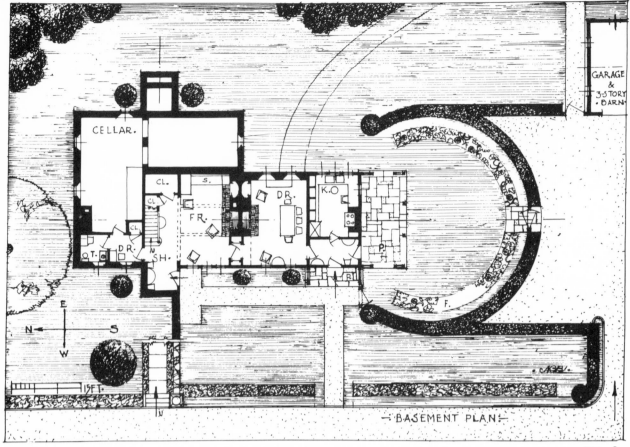

GARAGE & 3 STORY BARN

CELLAR.

CL.
CL.
CL.
DR.
T.C.
SH.
FR.
S.
DR.
K.O
P.
B.

N E S W

15 FT.

−·BASEMENT PLAN·−

NO. 80

ℭHE YOUNG HOUSE

Chatham Center, New York   Original Built 1810–15

Drawing No. 80   "The Young House" at Chatham Center, New York, was built at a period just before the Greek Revival and fifty years or more after the Dutch Houses of the Hudson River Valley were built. Such houses were usually built of stone or brick. The Young House, as are so many of this period, is a farmer's house and an excellent illustration of how farmers lived at that period. The original of this house which belongs to one of the author's daughters has a gable and lean-to roof and was built in the years about 1810 to 1815. It has interesting decoration at the corners around the windows of the Main Section which gave the house a touch of the days to come.

This farmer's house of frame is built on a hill which slopes to the south with the lower Stair Hall, Family Room, and Dining Room with fireplaces, Kitchen and Porch all above ground on this lower level with a circular, hedged

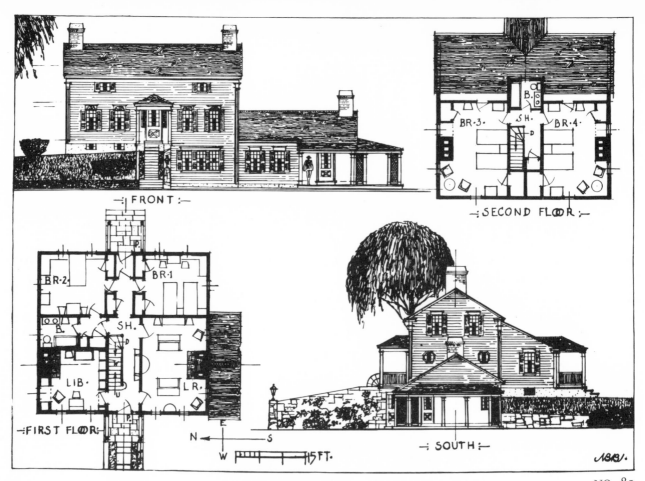

FRONT

SECOND FLOOR

BR·3   B.   BR·4
        SH.
        D

FIRST FLOOR

BR·2   BR·1
B.   SH.
LIB.   LR.

N   E
W   S
15 FT.

SOUTH

NO. 81

PERSPECTIVE

NO. 82

Garden at the Porch end. The author has taken the liberty on paper of bringing the barn and live stock quarters and farm uphill to the house location for convenience, in place of down hill and across the road where it now stands.

Thus, up to this point, the author has described the Basement Plan, Drawing No. 80. You will note the large space devoted to farmer's storage.

Drawing No. 81 This drawing is the First Floor Plan of the Main Unit of the house which is reached from the Basement Stairs inside and from the outside by a long flight of stone steps up the hill as indicated. The plan shows a Stair Hall through the Main Unit with an outside doorway and decorative Porch at the upper level on the east side overlooking the property and farm. On this floor is a Library and a Living Room which can be turned into a Bedroom if desired. A Stair Hall leads to the Second Floor.

This drawing shows the Second Floor Plan including the Stair Hall, two Bedrooms and a Bath. It also shows a drawing of the entire front or south elevation, drawn to scale as indicated.

Drawing No. 82 This drawing is a perspective indicating the house, barn and farmland with the tillable ground easily accessible for crops—a well-coordinated farm group.

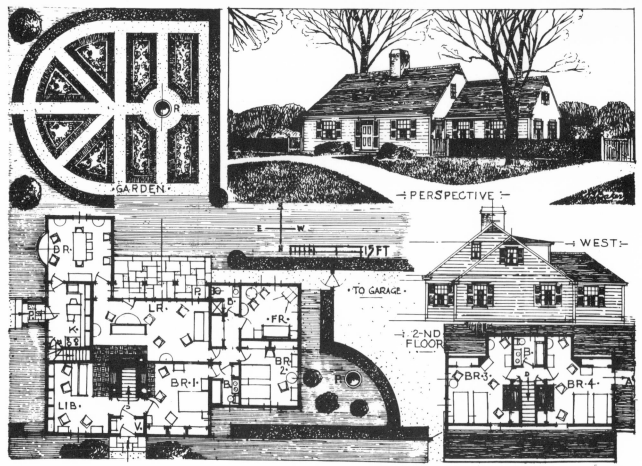

GARDEN

PERSPECTIVE

WEST

E · W

15 FT

TO GARGE

·2·ND FLOOR·

BR·

LR·

K·

LIB·

BR·1·

B·

V·

FR·

BR· 2·

R·

BR·3·

B·

BR·4·

A·

NO. 83

CAPE COD HOUSE

Little Point St., Essex, Connecticut   Original Built 1800

Drawing No. 83

This drawing shows the First and Second Floor plans of a very compact Single-Chimney, Gable-Roof, Cape Cod House which is located on Little Point Street in Essex, Connecticut. The author has made several changes but the type remains the same. The Essex house has four windows on the road front instead of the two that the author has used and a two Bedroom Wing has been added on the northwest end.

The First Floor Plan is as follows: From the private drive one enters a Vestibule leading to a small Stair Hall. On the east side one enters the Library and through this a large Living Room with Porch and Terrace. From the Living Room to the southeast is the Dining Room and between the Dining Room and the Library is located the Kitchen with a covered Porch to the outside on the east.

The Living Room and Dining Room both overlook the Garden. To the right or west of the Stair Hall is located Bedroom No. 1 and the Bedroom Wing composed of Bedroom No. 2, Family Room and two Bathrooms. Fireplaces are provided in the Library, Living Room, and Bedroom No. 1.

The Second Floor Plan is composed of Bedrooms No. 3 and No. 4 and a Bathroom. Space "A" off Bedroom No. 4 and the upper part of the Wing could be made into a Playroom if so desired. There are fireplaces in Bedrooms No. 3 and No. 4.

The drawing also contains a perspective view of the exterior of the house taken from the northwest indicating the location of the house on the property and the landscaping.

The Garage is separate and not shown.

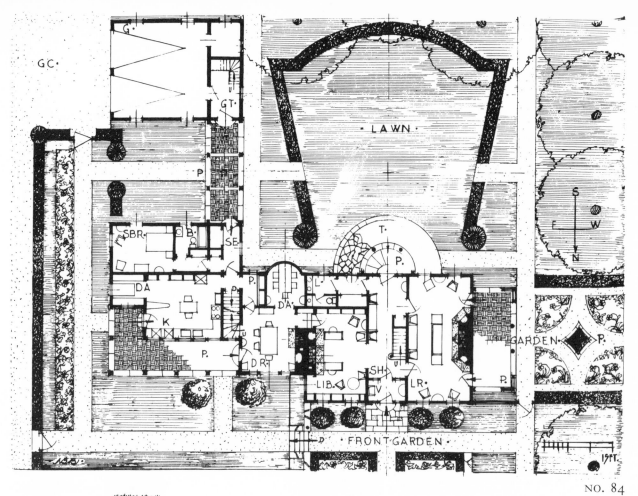

LAWN

GC.

G.

GT.

SBR. B. SE.

DA.

K.

DR.

P. P.

DA.

LIB. SH. V. LR.

GARDEN P.

FRONT GARDEN

15FT.

NO. 84

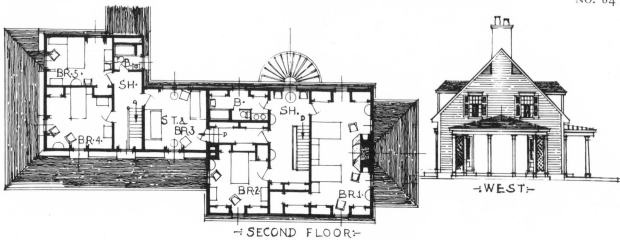

BR.5

B.

SH.

BR.4

ST. & BR.3

B.

SH.

BR.2

BR.1

SECOND FLOOR

WEST

EAST ELEVATION

NO. 85

EAST MARION FARMHOUSE

East Marion, L.I., New York   Original Built 1800

Drawing No. 84 This house inspired by an "Old Farm House" in East Marion, Long Island, New York, is of frame construction and L-shaped. The building ties in with a two-car Garage and an open Arcade to the Garden.

The First Floor Plan is as follows: The Main Unit contains a Vestibule Entrance from an unusual front Garden as indicated on Drawing No. 86. From the Vestibule one enters a wide Stair Hall and to the west a large Living Room with a Porch opening out on a Pool and Garden. At the south end of the Stair Hall is a small, round Porch with a paved Terrace overlooking a lawn hedge surrounded and approached from the north, east, and west. To the east of the Stair Hall is a large Library leading to the Dining Room, Dining Alcove, Lavatory, and Coat Room. Fireplaces are provided as indicated.

In a two-story Wing with a Basement, besides the Dining Room and Pantry the Wing contains a second flight of Stairs to the Second Floor and Basement, a Kitchen and Dining Alcove, a long Porch and Servant's Bedroom and Bath. From this Wing to the south is an open Arcade to the south Gardens. This also leads to a two-car Garage. The landscaping is as indicated.

Drawing No. 85 This drawing contains a Second Floor Plan with four Bedrooms and a combination Bedroom and Study and two Stair Halls. A fireplace is provided in the large west Bedroom. Two Bathrooms are as indicated.

This drawing also contains east and west exterior elevations drawn to scale.

NO. 86

Drawing No. 86 This drawing is a perspective of the house exterior showing house, property and landscaping.

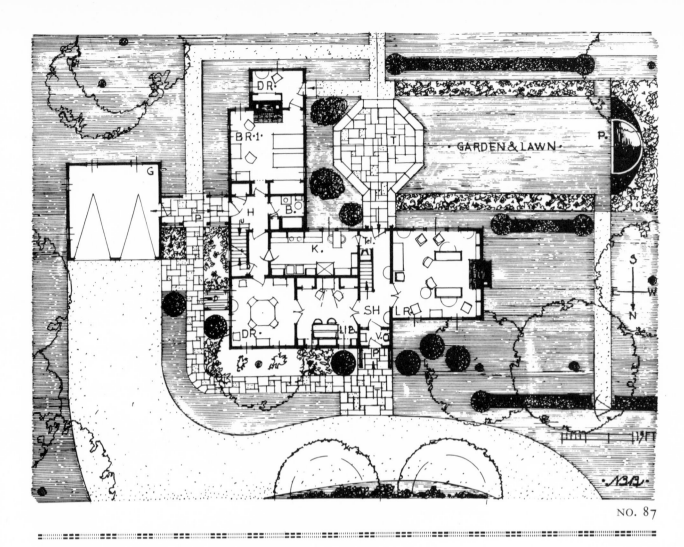

THE FALK HOUSE

Greenlawn, L.I., New York   Original Built 1800

Drawing No. 87   This house, owned by one of the author's daughters and her husband and called the Falk House on the plan, was inspired by "The Clock House" in Bay Shore, Long Island, New York. The exact date of construction of the older parts of the house is unknown to the author but it is said to have been built about 1800. The author reproduced the "Clock House," with minor changes, to suit a wooded hillside site on a part of his own property. The Falk House is placed on a level part of this property with a wooded hill planted with wild flowers behind the house as a background.

This drawing is the First Floor Plan and the main section of the house. It shows the entrance door opening to a Stair Hall with a wide doorway to the left or east, opening to a Library and, beyond, a Dining Room. A stairway with a decorative open rail leads to the Second Floor with a balcony above.

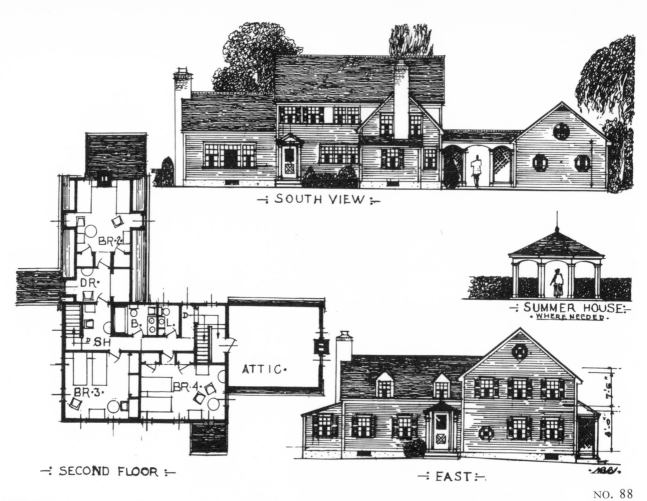

—: SOUTH VIEW :—

—: SUMMER HOUSE :—
· WHERE NEEDED ·

BR·2·

DR·

B.   CL.

SH

BR·3·   BR·4·

ATTIC.

—: SECOND FLOOR :—

—: EAST :—

NO. 88

—: PERSPECTIVE :—

NO. 89

To the south is the Kitchen with a southerly door from the Main Stair Hall. The Hall, as planned, opens on the south to a paved Terrace with Summer House. A part of the east Stair Hall is shown and a Side Arcade Entrance to a two-car Garage. Bedroom No. 1, a Bathroom and a Dressing Room complete the plan of the First Floor of the southerly Wing. A fireplace in Bedroom No. 1 is provided. To the west of the Main Stair Hall is a Living Room Wing one and one-half stories high with a fireplace and a large window overlooking the Garden Terrace and planted hill beyond.

In the view from the southerly Terrace there is planned by the author a large hedge-surrounded Pool, and a hedged-in Garden.

Drawing No. 88 This drawing is the Second Floor Plan and contains three Bedrooms, two Bathrooms, a Dressing Room and Stair Hall as indicated and a large, floored-over space over the Living Room on the First Floor.

Drawing No. 89 This drawing contains a perspective view of the exterior of the House, Garage, and Connecting Arcade showing the site landscaping and the hill to the south.

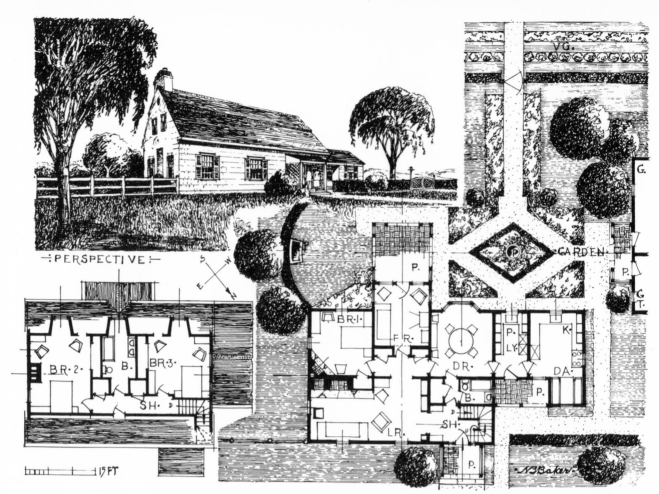

-PERSPECTIVE-

15 FT

N J Baker

NO. 90

THE GARDEN CITY FARMHOUSE

Garden City, L.I., New York   Original Built 1800

Drawing No. 90   Those of you who remember when the country lay just outside your town or city can also remember how you looked across a field to the nearest house barely visible among the trees. A little way off was the barn, and cows waited in the meadows. Such a house was the "Garden City Farmhouse" which inspired this modernized version.

The First Floor Plan includes an Entrance Porch from a private road. The door opens to a Stair Hall with stairway to the Basement and Second Floor. The plan includes a Living Room, Dining Room, Kitchen, Dining Alcove, Pantry and Bedroom No. 1; also, First Floor Bath, Family Room, and Porch overlooking the Garden.

The flower and vegetable gardens are shown and of course a two-car Garage and Garden tool room.

The Second Floor contains two Bedrooms and adjoining Bathrooms besides the Stair Hall.

The drawing contains, as well, an outside perspective view of the house as one saw it one hundred years ago, neighbors out of sight with only fields and landscape in the picture.

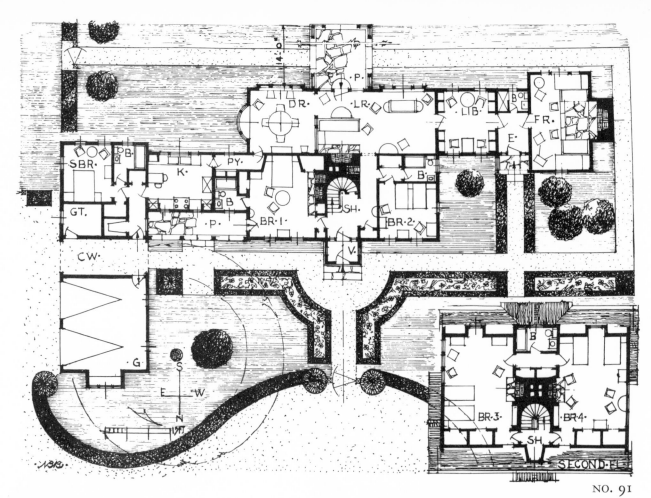

PERSPECTIVE

P.

DR. LR. LIB. FR.

SBR. B. E.

GT. K. PY. B. BR. 2.

CW. P. BR. 1. SH. V.

G. BR. 3. BR. 4.

S N E W SH. SECOND FL.

NO. 91

PERSPECTIVE

NO. 92

A LONG CAPE COD HOUSE

Cape Cod, Massachusetts   Original Built 1800

Drawing No. 91   The main, central-chimney unit with the "break-your-back" windows of a narrow Cape Cod house was the inspiration for this drawing. A house with this type of windows is hard to find and this particular central unit with such windows is of fine proportions. This house was discovered by the author and his wife on the Cape on one of many trips by car through New England. It is an exquisite Long Cape Cod House with a Long Ridge Pole and break-your-back Windows on the Second Floor. The author has used it as a central feature for this long house, the longer part of which is only one story in height.

The central unit, First Floor Plan shows a Vestibule Entrance from a private road. From this Entrance of the main, two-story unit, to the east and west are Bedrooms No. 1 and No. 2 with Bathrooms. One Bedroom has a fireplace. A Dining Room is shown to the southeast and a large Porch from the Living Room to the south.

In a one-story Wing to the west is a Library, a separate Entrance with a Porch, a large Family Room with fireplace, built-in seats and bunk beds for guests.

In a one-story Wing to the east is located a Pantry, Kitchen and Porch Entrance as well as a Servant's Bedroom and Bath. To the north is a Covered Entrance from the Garage Court and a two-car Garage.

The Second Floor Plan of the Central Main Unit shows two large Bedrooms with connecting Bathroom and fireplaces. Stair Hall is as indicated.

Drawing No. 92   This drawing is a perspective of the house and surrounding landscaping. The development of grounds is an indication of what can be done and is purely the imagination of the author.

SECOND FLOOR.

DR.

B.

BR.2.   BR.3.

P.

P.   K.

DR.   P.   B.

LR.   SH.   BR.1.

GARDEN   P.

GT.

G.

PERSPECTIVE.

S
E   W
N

NO. 93

THE OLD STARKEY HOUSE

Essex, Connecticut   Original Built 1800

Drawing No. 93   This drawing is that of a small house with gambrel roof and central chimney and enclosed by a decorative fence. It is on Main Street, Essex, Connecticut, and is opposite the old hotel and famous eating place of the town. This "Old Starkey House" is the inspiration for this house drawing. Essex is a wonderful old town with fine old houses and old family names such as the Lays, Haydens, Pratts, Lewises, Hinghams, and the Starkeys, all British in origin and settlers of the town of Essex.

The author designed a house on West Avenue which sits between two famous houses at least a century or so old.

The First Floor Plan is a simple one but, although compact, it is spacious in effect. Coming in off the street, one steps into an Entrance Hall and Stairs to the Second Floor. Turning to the left or east, one enters the Living Room the width of the house which opens to the Dining Room. To the south is the Kitchen, Pantry and a Porch. To the right of the Stair Hall or west, one enters the downstairs Bedroom No. 1 and Bath. Three rooms have fireplaces opening on a central chimney. In a one-story addition there is a stairway to the Basement and an outside Porch leading to a one-car Garage. Nearby is a Garden with fountain seen from the front. There is also a small Garden with Pool to the south.

The Second Floor Plan has two large Bedrooms No. 2 and No. 3, Bathroom and Stair Hall with a Dressing Room off Bedroom No. 3, all as indicated. Both Bedrooms have fireplaces.

The perspective view is of the house and the author's idea of the landscaping and general arrangement of the property.

PERSPECTIVE

SECOND FLOOR

W
S — N
E

NO. 94

27 MAIN ST.

Essex, Connecticut   Original Built 1800

Drawing No. 94   The inspiration for the house on this drawing is known as "Number 27 Main Street" in Essex, Connecticut. At the present time, it has been partly covered up with another building but the author has always admired this house in particular.

It is a small cottage but compact. The building is a gambrel-roof, single-central-chimney type with a lean-to.

The First Floor Plan has an Entrance Hall facing south. To the west of the Entrance is Bedroom No. 1 and to the east is a Living Room with a Dining Room off to its north. From the Dining Room one enters a Covered Porch and from this to the north is a connecting one-car Garage. West of the Dining Room is a small but compact Kitchen. Also to the west is a Bathroom, Sitting Room, another Bedroom and Stair Hall.

The Second Floor Plan contains two Bedrooms, a Bathroom with shower, and a Stair Hall.

Although it is a little house, it is beautiful to look at and has a convenient plan to live with.

On the same drawing is a perspective view of the house, the front facing the south and enclosed with trimmed hedges. This perspective is drawn at a larger scale and shows the location on the west side of the road. On all sides of the house are Garden areas.

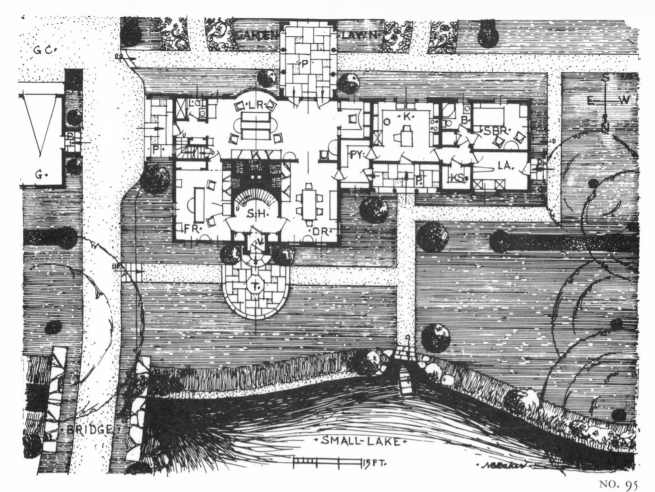

NO. 95

PERSPECTIVE

SECOND·FLOOR

EAST FRONT

NO. 96

THE DEAN-BARSTON HOUSE

East Taunton, Massachusetts   Original Built 1800

Drawing No. 95 The drawing of this house was inspired by "The Deane-Barston House" of East Taunton, Masschusetts. It is a single, central-chimney, gable-roof type of frame construction. The site located was fixed by the author, who, having seen a similar site, chose it for this house. A private road with a stone bridge at the entrance covers a stream which provides the water for the pond in front of the house. The road turns off to a two-car Garage with a Side Entrance to the house. The original house was built in 1800, the period when the Greek Revival was at its best. However, this house does not show the Greek Revival influence.

The First Floor Plan shows the front of the house facing the pond. The house Entrance is through a Vestibule opening from a stone-paved Terrace. From the Vestibule one enters the Stair Hall and to the left or east side, the Family Room is located. To the south of the Famiiy Room is a large Living Room with stairs to the Second Floor, a Lavatory, and a small Porch. Off the Living Room there is a large Porch leading to a circular, hedged-in Garden and lawn.

From the Stair Hall to the west there is a spacious Dining Room. Fireplaces are provided for the three rooms of the Main House.

To the right or west of the Main House is a one-story Wing containing a small Library off the Living Room, a Pantry and Kitchen Stores, Servant's Bedroom and Bath.

Drawing No. 96 This drawing contains a Second Floor Plan with a front and rear Stair Hall, four Bedrooms and two Bathrooms, and a stairway to the Attic.

The drawing also shows the east Front, drawn to scale, and a perspective showing a possible location of the house near the Pond and the surrounding landscape and country.

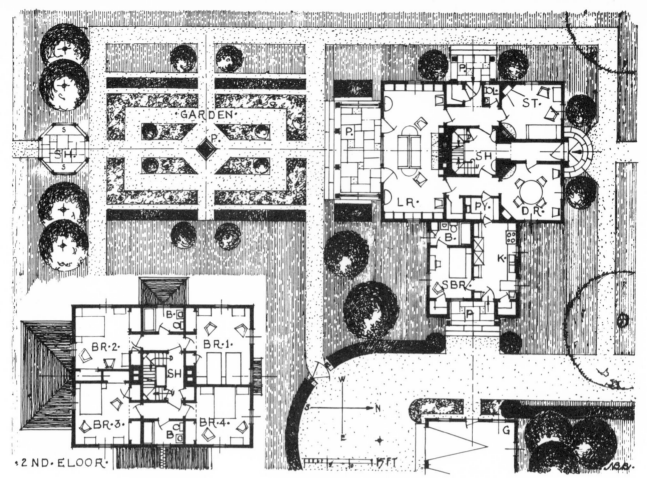

GARDEN

2ND·FLOOR·

NO. 97

—: PERSPECTIVE :—

NO. 98

THE HOUSE IN WINDSOR

Windsor, Connecticut　　　　　　　　Original Built 1825

Drawing No. 97　The inspiration for this drawing is "The House in Windsor" one of the River towns of Connecticut. The name of the original owner is not known to the author. It is a beautiful house. The pediment of the simple, classical front faces the north with central entrance from a private road.

The south face overlooks the Garden and summer house from a large Porch of classical design.

The main part of the house on the First Floor has a Living Room the full width of the house on the south, a Dining Room, and Sitting Room on Front or north. The Stair Hall in the center leads to the Second Floor and Basement. The Entrance Porch on the west opens to a second door to the Living Room and a Lavatory.

A one-story Addition containing a Kitchen, Servant's Bedroom and Bath, and small Porch was added by the author, as well as a two-car Garage and Service Court. The formal Garden is to be enjoyed from the Porch on the southern end and a small summer house on axis with it. The Garden will allow extension to the area, if desired.

The Second Floor Plan contains four Bedrooms and two Bathrooms and central Stair Hall which completes the plan.

Drawing No. 98　This drawing is a perspective of the exterior of the house, Addition and Garage, located by the author on a level plain with low hills in the distance.

The date of the construction of the original house was given to the author locally, in Windsor, as 1825.

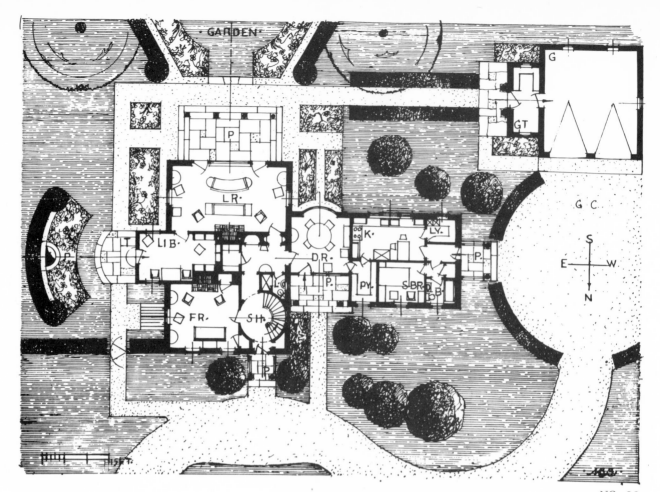

GARDEN

G

GT

G C

S
E — W
N

LR.

LIB.

DR.

K.

LY.

P.

P.

P.

FR.

SH.

L.

P.

PY.

S·BR·

B.

B.

P.

NO. 99

—:PERSPECTIVE:—

—:SECOND
FLOOR:—

BR·1·

B.

BR·2·

SH·

B.

BR·3·

NO. 100

THE SWIFT HOUSE

Oxford, New Hampshire   Original Built 1825

Drawing No. 99   These drawings are inspired by "The Swift House" at Oxford, New Hampshire, which is entirely different from any house in that town. Its walls were built of brick and it is assumed that they were furred on the inside. The front gable end faces the road and the rear gable is the same but could be of frame construction, stuccoed or brick veneered, as desired.

The First Floor Plan has been increased in length by the author and by introducing a one-story Wing provides for a Dining Room and Kitchen, a Servant's Room, and Bath. The Garage is separate, as indicated. On the west side of the Main House is an Entrance Porch and inside is a circular Stair Hall. Opposite the Hall is a Family Room with a fireplace. This room can be used as a spare Bedroom with Lavatory across the Hall. At the south end of the house is a large Living Room with a fireplace and paved Porch overlooking the Garden and lawn. To the east between the Living Room and Family Room is located a small Library with outside Terrace and small semi-circular Garden, hedge, and Pool.

Drawing No. 100   This drawing contains the Second Floor Plan with Three Bedrooms and two Bathrooms, and a pull-down stairs to the Attic.

A perspective of the exterior of the house from the north finishes this drawing together with the landscaping and private road approach.

SUN DECK

BR·3· BR·4·
B B
BR·1· BR·2·

·2ND FLOOR·

·P·

·LR·
·F·

·G·
·P·
·B·
·K·
·S·BR·
·SH·
·PY·
·B·
·FR·
·DR·
·H·

·DRIVE

·P·

·P·

GARDEN·

GARDEN·

·ORCHARD·

15 FT
·A.B.Baker·

N

NO. 101

THE BALDWIN HOUSE

Audubon, New York   Original Built 1830

Drawing No. 101 This drawing is inspired by "The Baldwin House" of Audubon, New York. It is one of the earliest of the Greek Revival houses in the state of New York. The Greek Revival was of short duration, but though extending only from about 1820 to 1850, during this period both public buildings and dwellings conformed to this style. This was general throughout the country even though the period was short.

This drawing includes the First and Second Floor Plans and a perspective of the exterior with landscaping as indicated. This is a frame-constructed building. The house is composed of a two-story, Central Unit with pediment and two-story column and Porch on north front and pediment on south front where a half-circle Porch with columns is located. This Porch is one-story high. The east and west Wings are also one story high. A separate one-story Garage to the east of the house is as indicated.

The plan for the Central Section on the First Floor contains the Entrance and Long Hall to the Stair Hall. The Living Room is the full width of the Wing with circular Porch on the south overlooking the grounds. A Dining Room, circular Stair Hall, Pantry and small Library are in the Central Wing.

To the right or west is a Wing housing a pleasant Family Room and a Lavatory. To the left or east end is a Wing containing a Kitchen, Servant's Bedroom and Bath, and a small Porch. East of the driveway is located a two-car Garage.

The Second Floor Plan includes four Bedrooms, two Bathrooms, and circular Stair Hall and a Sun Deck.

This drawing also contains a perspective drawing of the exterior of the house taken from the north with the landscaping around the house.

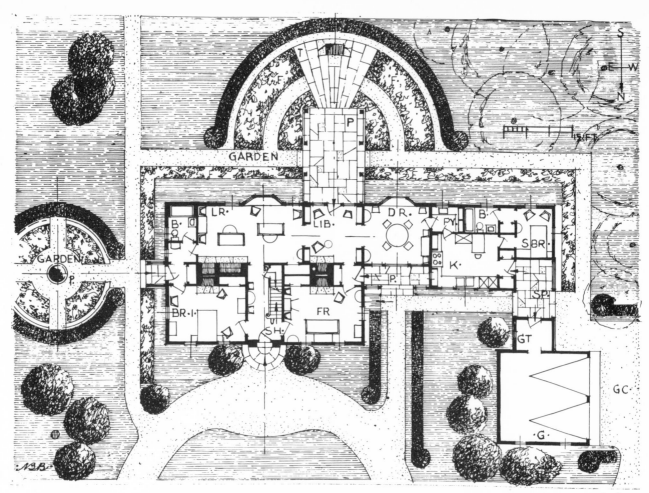

GARDEN

GARDEN

LR.

LIB.

DR.

B.

S BR.

K.

BR·1·

FR

SH·

SP.

GT

GC

G

NO. 102

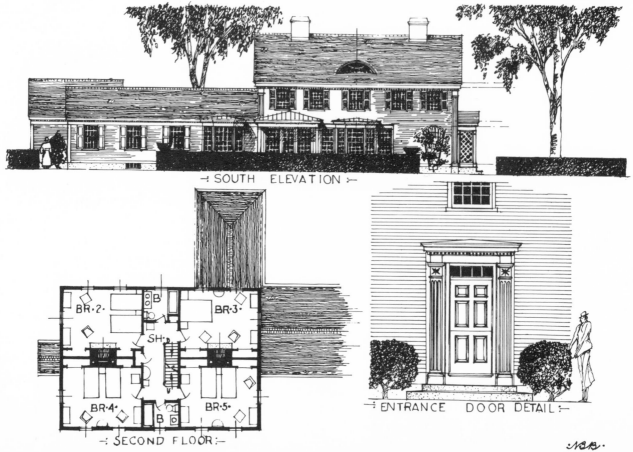

⊢ SOUTH ELEVATION ⊣

BR·2·

B.

BR·3·

SH·

BR·4·

BR·5·

B

⊢ SECOND FLOOR ⊣

⊢ ENTRANCE DOOR DETAIL ⊣

NO. 103

THE PENNY LINCOLN HOUSE

Scotland, Connecticut   Original Built 1835

Drawing No. 102   All through the state of Connecticut are two-chimney, frame houses similar to "The Penny Lincoln House" in Scotland, Connecticut, which inspired this house. Through Windham County there are many like it, spacious and symmetrical and characteristic in type of northeastern Connecticut as the one-chimney type is of central and western Connecticut.

     The First Floor Plan of this drawing consists of a Main House Unit with a private road leading to the Main Entrance. Inside is a central Stair Hall leading to a large Living Room to the south with a Lavatory and with a Side Entrance on the east side. This leads to a round, hedged-in Garden with a Pool. At the west end is a Library opening onto a large, paved Porch and a semi-circular Garden with a paved, open grill area for barbecues. In the house on the northeast side of the Stair Hall is a large Bedroom with Bath. Across the side Hall and to the northeast of the Stair Hall is located a Family Room. All rooms in the Main Unit have fireplaces.

     To the west the author has indicated a one-story Wing containing a Dining Room and Porch, a Pantry, Kitchen, Servant's Room and Bath, also a Service Porch, and two-car Garage to the north.

Drawing No. 103   This drawing contains a Second Floor Plan with four, equal-sized Bedrooms with fireplaces, two Bathrooms, and a Stair Hall.

     The drawing also shows the south elevation and Entrance Door detail.

-: PERSPECTIVE :-

NO. 104

Drawing No. 104　This drawing contains a perspective view of the exterior of the house and landscaping of barn and farm. The outgoing boats, river, and surrounding terrain are imaginary.

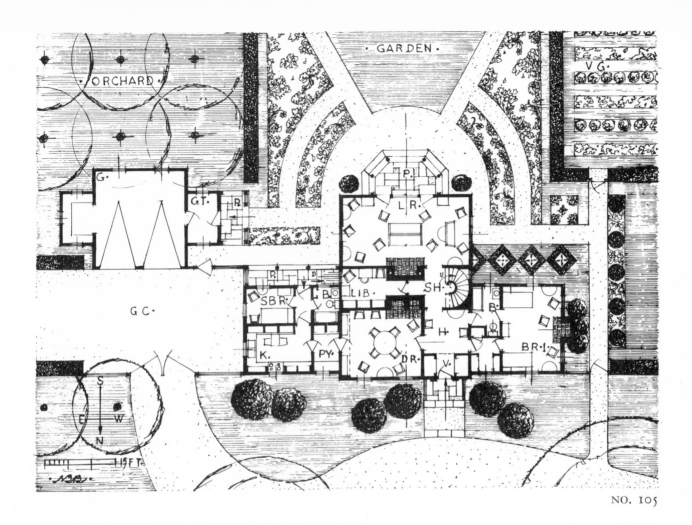

House at Lyme

Lyme, Connecticut   Original Built 1800

Drawing No. 105 The house that inspired the author to make these drawings is one in the residential part of Lyme, Connecticut. It is a beautiful, long house with classical lines and detail and it is on axis with one of the old streets of Lyme. The author and his wife have seen almost its counterpart in "The Peyton Randolph" house in Williamsburg, Virginia.

The First Floor Plan of this house starts from a private drive and an Entrance Vestibule on the right side of the central unit. This opens to a circular Hall from which one enters a Dining Room with fireplace, a small Library, and a large Living Room. A Porch on the southerly end looks out on a formal Garden and lawn enclosed with clipped hedges.

To the west of the Entrance Hall is a one-story Wing with a Bedroom with fireplace and Bathroom. To the east is a one-story Wing containing a Kitchen,

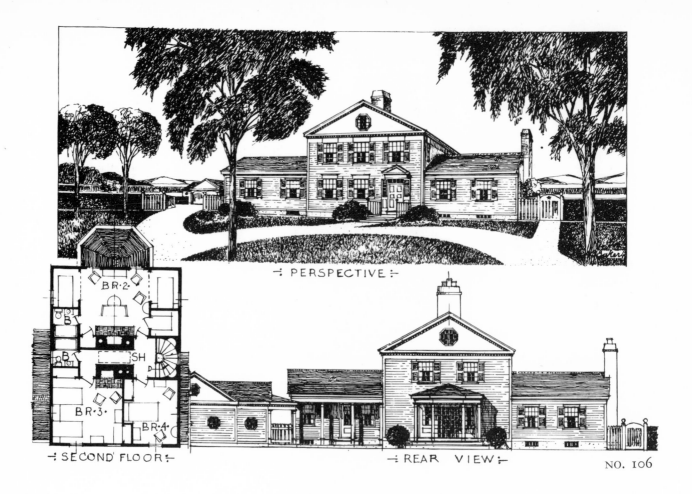

‐: PERSPECTIVE :‐

‐: SECOND FLOOR :‐

‐: REAR VIEW :‐

NO. 106

Pantry, Servant's Bedroom and Bath, and Service Porch. To the east is a separate two-car Garage with accessory structures.

Drawing No. 106 This drawing shows a Second Floor Plan of the Main Central Unit containing three Bedrooms and two Bathrooms with fireplaces in Bedrooms No. 2 and No. 3, a circular Stair Hall, and a pull-down stairs to the Attic.

This drawing also includes a Rear Elevation of the house drawn to scale and a prespective view of the north exterior of the house and landscaping.

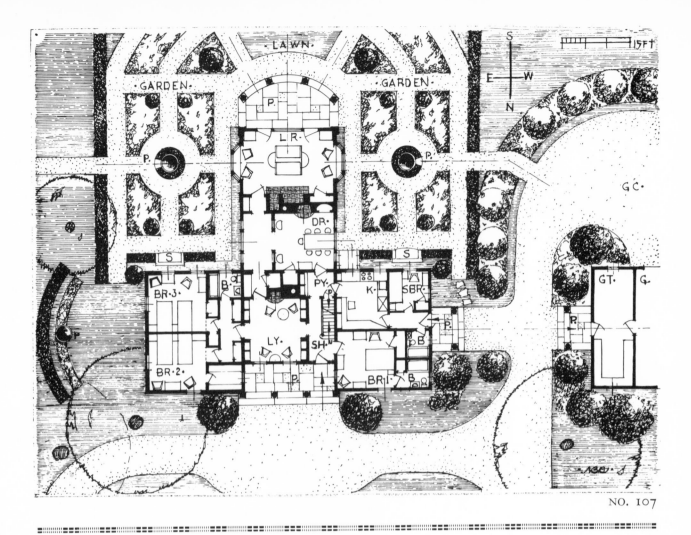

NO. 107

JUDGE BINGHAM HOUSE

West Cornwall, Vermont　　　　Original Built 1843

Drawing No. 107　　This drawing is the First Floor Plan of a house surrounded by decorative Gardens. On the west side a two-car Garage has been added with the parking area to the south planted with a ring of fruit trees.

The First Floor Plan shows the Central Wing to be two stories high with a columned Porch the full height. One enters from the Porch to a Stair Hall on the west end and proceeds through the Library to the Dining Room and beyond to the Living Room, all three of which have fireplaces. At the south end of the Living Room a large semi-circular Porch gives a wonderful view of the Gardens laid out as indicated. From the Library to the east is a one-story Wing which contains two Bedrooms and a Bath. On the west in a one-story Wing is located another Bedroom and Bath, a Kitchen and Pantry, Servant's Bedroom and Bath.

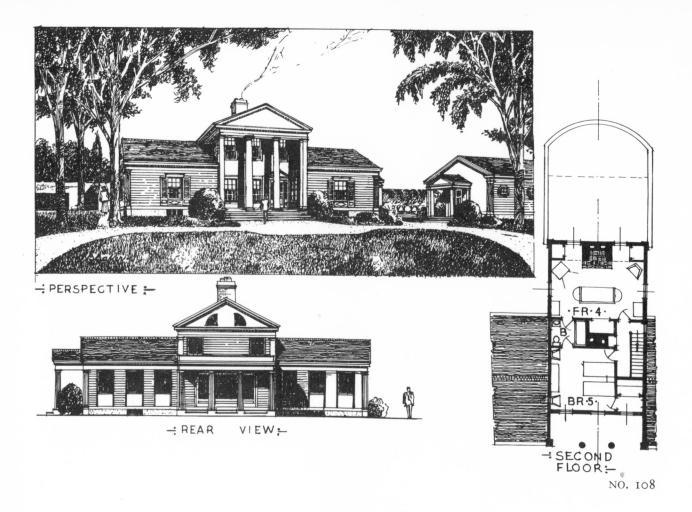

-: PERSPECTIVE :-

-: REAR VIEW :-

FR·4·

BR·5·

-: SECOND FLOOR :-

NO. 108

Drawing No. 108   This drawing contains the plan of the Second Floor of the Central Wing and this provides a Bedroom and Bath, and a Family Room with a large deck for a Sitting Area out of doors, as indicated.

This drawing also contains a Rear Elevation drawn to scale and a perspective view of the entire house and Garage together with the surrounding landscape.

This house is of Greek Revival style and was inspired by "The Judge Bingham House" of West Cornwall, Vermont.

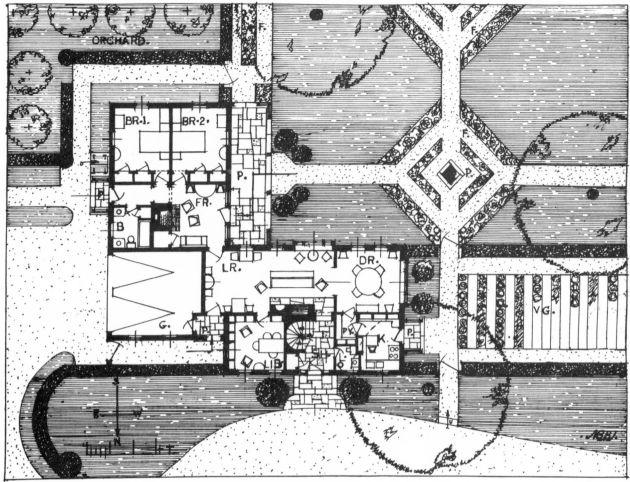

BRICK GAMBREL HOUSE

Farmingham, Connecticut   Original Built 1845

Drawing No. 109   The inspiration for this house is a brick, Gambrel-Roof House the author saw in Farmington, Connecticut, and the original owner's name is not known to him and could not be found by him locally.

The First Floor Plan is as follows: From a private road, an Entrance Door with flush side lights leads into a rounded, paved Stair Hall to the Second Floor and to a Living Room on the south side. The Living Room has a fireplace and a large bay window. To the right or southwest side is a Dining Room and on the north is the Kitchen and a Lavatory opening off the Stair Hall.

From the long Living Room on the northeast end is a Library and a small Entrance to the house. A two-car Garage is provided.

On the southeast end of the Living Room an opening leads to a Family

‐: PERSPECTIVE :‐

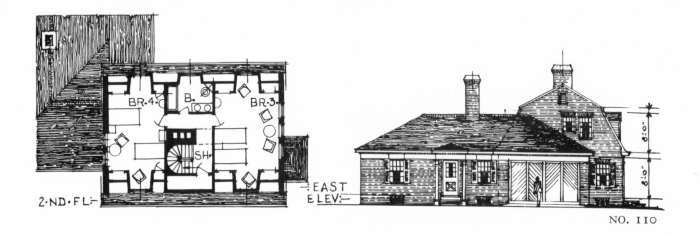

2·ND·FL·

‐: EAST
ELEV:‐

NO. 110

Room with a long Porch looking out on a flower and vegetable garden, as indicated.

The room is provided with a fireplace. Off the Family Room are two Bedrooms, a Bathroom, and East Entrance.

Drawing No. 110 This drawing contains the Second Floor of the main section of the house running east and west, two Bedrooms the width of the house, a Bathroom, and a Stair Hall.

The drawing also contains an east elevation of the wing and Main House drawn to scale and a perspective view of the house from the outside showing the landscaping.

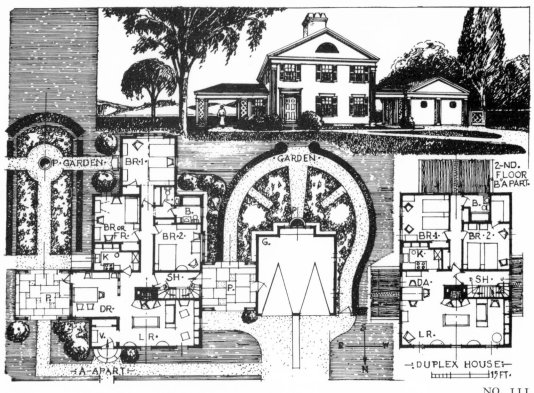

Two FAMILY HOUSE WITH GARDEN

by Author

Drawing No. III This drawing shows two separate Apartments in one house—a paying proposition if one can build the extra apartment upstairs at the same time. If not, at least the roughing for the plumbing, heating, and electrical work for upstairs fireplace, if desired, can be provided and the other work done at a later date with minimum disturbance.

It has the appearance of a single house and is a good investment. The First Floor Apartment has a Front Entrance from a private road. From the Vestibule one enters the large Living Room, opening to the Dining Room, compact Kitchen, and three Bedrooms and Bathroom. The Stair Hall is a common entrance for both apartments. The First Floor apartment has a private Porch overlooking the Garden. The Garage is common to both.

The upstairs apartment is entered through the west Porch doorway and the Garden to the west belongs to the Upstairs Apartment. This apartment has a large Living Room with fireplace, a Dining Alcove, a Kitchen, and two Bedrooms and a Bathroom. A pull-down staircase in the Stair Hall can serve both apartments for storage.

A Basement is under the house area.

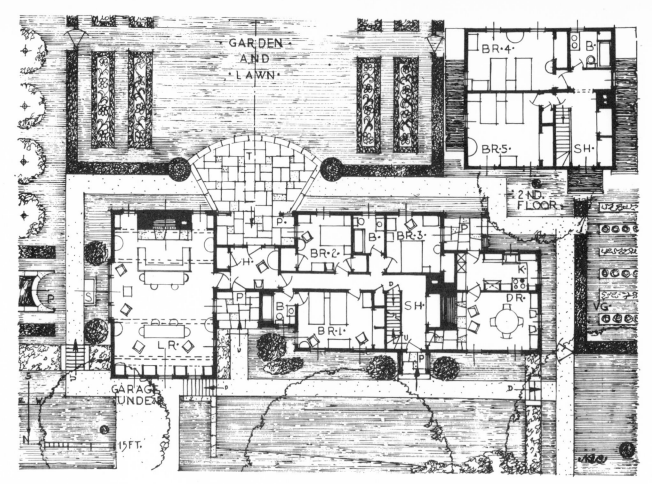

GARDEN
AND
LAWN

BR·4·

B·

BR·5·

SH·

2ND.
FLOOR

P·

B·

BR·3·

BR·2·

P·

H·

K·

P·

B·

SH·

DR·

VG·

BR·1·

S·

P·

LR·

P·

GARAGE
UNDER

N

15 FT.

NO. 112

-: PERSPECTIVE :-

NO. 113

A LONG HOUSE CONNECTED TO BARN
by Author

Drawing No. 112   This drawing contains the First and Second Floor Plans of A Long House Connected to an Existing Barn. The author has seen this or a similar house in his travels somewhere through New England.

The First Floor Plan starts with the Barn because the Garage is under it and the large Living Room with fireplace above it.

From a private road to a parking space north of the Garage but not shown, one walks up a few steps to the Entrance Porch and from here into the house by way of the Entrance Hall. At the left or east, the large Living Room is entered and to the right or west the long Hall leads to a westerly Entrance Hall, Dining Room, and Kitchen.

Beyond is a Bedroom Wing with three Bedrooms and two Bathrooms. At the east Entrance there is a paved Porch and large paved Terrace leading to a Garden outlined with hedge, flower beds and lawn.

The Dining Room to the west has a large fireplace and the Kitchen to the south has a Service Porch.

On the Second Floor Plan there are two large Bedrooms and a Bathroom and Stair Hall.

Drawing No. 113   This drawing is given over entirely to a perspective view of the outside of the house taken from the northwest showing the site and the landscaping.

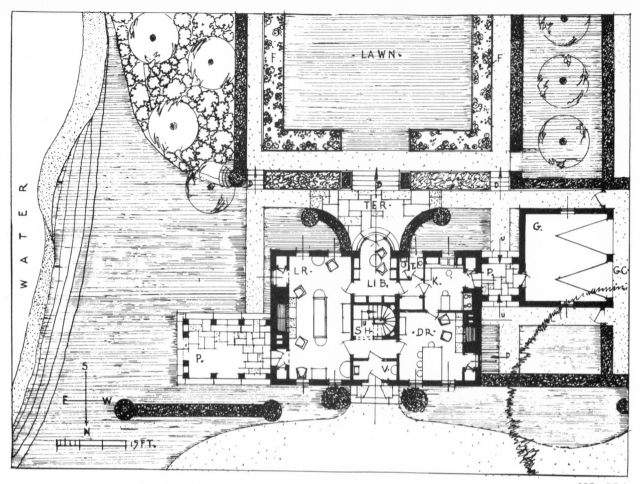

· LAWN ·

WATER

NO. 114

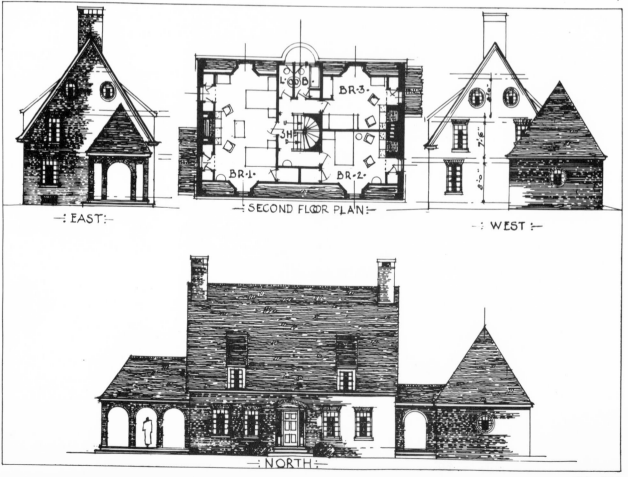

-: EAST :-   · SECOND FLOOR PLAN ·   -: WEST :-

- NORTH -

NO. 115

HUDSON RIVER VALLEY BRICK HOUSE
by Author

Drawing No. 114

This drawing is the First Floor Plan of a Hudson River Valley Brick House with High-Pitched Roof.

The river valley has many such houses built of brick and some of stone. The Dutch were very sturdy people and built well and thoroughly.

The house of "Hendrick Bries" built in Reneselaer County of New York State was built about 1722 and is one of the best examples of a steep-pitched-roof house. This house was inspired by the Bries house.

The house of this drawing is on the river's edge and faces the north. From a private road one enters a Vestibule and, from thence to the east, a large Living Room with a fireplace. This leads to a large Porch giving an expansive view of the Hudson River where the author has seen fit to place this sturdy house, as many of them are so placed. To the west of the entry is a large Dining Room with fireplace, directly south of the Entrance Vestibule the small Hall is a Stair Hall leading to the Second Floor and tall storage Attic. From the southwest end of the Living Room is a Library with a large outside paved Terrace with steps leading down to a rectangular Garden and orchard at the west side. West of the Library is a Lavatory and a large Coat Closet and entrance to Kitchen; also a door to the Dining Room and on the west a Service Porch and a two-car Carage and paved Court.

Drawing No. 115

This drawing contains a plan of the Second Floor with one large Bedroom and two smaller Bedrooms, all with fireplaces, a Stair Hall leading up to the Attic, and a Bathroom and separate Lavatory, as indicated.

The drawing also contains the north or Front Elevation and the Elevations of east and west, all drawn to scale.

NO. 116

Drawing No. 116 This drawing contains a perspective view of the house showing its location on the river. It also indicates some of the landscaping and the roads.

NO. 117

THE AUTHOR'S HOUSE

Greenlawn L.I., N.Y., by Author

Drawing No. 117 This drawing is the author's own house built with his own hands during his spare time and it is nice to think that possibly the author's ancestors did the same thing.

It also includes the landscaping and roads, none of which were originally there.

The house grew with the family in early American tradition with rooms added as needed, all of which are still needed for the children of another generation. Throughout is the author's handwork in carved moldings, stair rail, bookshelves, cabinets, etc. Pumpkin pine boarding for the living room and a paneled wall section with a mantelpiece and cupboards were brought from abandoned houses in New England. In 1930, quarry tile for a floor came from Wales and weathered three months on the way in a British tanker.

The house is built on what was once a secluded hilltop farm which gave it the name "High-Over." At that time it was a mile from the nearest village. Now with the village grown up to its property line, it is still secluded by landscaping that along with the house has come of age.